ICT in Higher Education

Dr.K. Dhanalakshmi

P. Manikandan

Published by

BONFRING®
Intellectual Integrity

ICT in Higher Education

ISBN 978-93-85477-95-9

Author

Dr.K. Dhanalakshmi

P. Manikandan

Bonfring

309, 2nd Floor, 5th Street Extension,

Gandhipuram, Coimbatore-641 012.

Tamilnadu, India.

E-mail: info@bonfring.org

Website: www.bonfring.org

Phone: 0422-3928700

Preface

A very important factor impelling change has been the technological explosion, particularly in the area of ICT. Such technologies are double-edged swords. They allow people to contact one another and exchange ideas very easily in order to create communities built around common interests and common causes. They also make it possible for global corporations to move billions of dollars around the world with the click of a button. The world is becoming increasingly homogenized. Shrinks on account of developments in science and technology, these changes affect. The world today is a global village, and this represents unprecedented challenges for Indian Education. No society can live in isolation. The centralization deprives teachers of the freedom to organize teaching learning and meaningfully participate in the preparation of syllabi or textbooks with the use of technology.

"Learning without Burden"-the report of the Yash Pal Committee(1993), has extensively reported on the ills of the present education system. Briefly, it has shown how the education system has become highly centralized, examination driven, joyless, impersonal, and utterly irrelevant to the child's world. But now in addition to what is happening in India, it has become necessary to face the challenges of a rapidly changing world in the twenty-first century. This technological process has been going on for the time, but in the last ten years the pace at which the world is changing is becoming greatly accelerated. Students must be motivated towards utilization of ICT for knowledge enhancement.

*This book covers the **Syllabus of TNTEU** for the students of B.Ed., and M.Ed., degree programmes.*

P. Manikandan

<table>
<tr><td>Chapter</td><td>Contents</td><td>Page No</td></tr>
</table>

Chapter	Contents	Page No
1	Educational Technology	1
	Definition	3
	Audio Visual Technology	3
	Technology in Education	4
	Technology Evaluation in Education	5
	Technology-Related Teacher Professional Development	6
	Integration of Technology into Teaching and Learning	8
	Student Technology Literacy	8
	AVRC	9
	EMMRC	10
	EDUSAT	11
	Countrywide Classrooms	12
	The Advantages and Disadvantages of Using ICT for Teaching and Learning	12
	How the Internet Enhances the Teaching Process	13
	Advantages of Students Using ICT for Learning	14
	Disadvantages of Using ICT for Education	16
	E-learning	17
	Open Educational Resources	20
	History of the Internet	23
	Internet and Education	23
	Critical Issues in Internet Usages	25
	Origins of the Internet	26
	Web Browser	27
2	Communication Technology in Education	29
	Concept	30
	Characteristics and Elements	30
	Characteristics of Communication	33
	Essentials of Communication Process	34
	Types of Communication	34
	Models of Communication	36
	Types of Classroom Communication	38

	Communication Network	39
	Barriers of Communication	45
	Factors Affecting Communication	46
	The Role and Influence of Mass Media	48
	Mass Media and Education	51
	Barriers and Solution	52
3	New Horizons in ICT	55
	Recent Trends in the Area of ICT	55
	Interactive Video	58
	Interactive White Board	60
	Video Conferencing	63
	M-Learning	65
	Social Media	68
	Community Radio	70
	Gyan Dharshan	71
	Gyan Vani	73
	Blog	74
	MOOC	74
	Whatsapp	76
	Twitter	76
	Virtual Classroom	78
	Blended Learning	82
	Flipped Classroom	83
	Cloud Computing	86
	Applications of ICT for Enriching Classroom	88
	10 Reasons to Use Multimedia in the Classroom	91
	Using Computer based Learning	93
	Collaborative Technology Learning	97
4	E-Content Development	99
	Meaning and Concept	99
	Advantages of Using E-Content	102
	Multimedia Elements of E-Content	103
	Phase of E-Content Development	108
	ADDIE Model	110

Characteristics of Multimedia Technology 112

Multimedia 113

Multimedia Package in Teacher Training 115

Multimedia Laboratory 116

PSI 118

Origin and Growth of PSI 120

Current Status of PSI 121

LCI 124

5 Organizing and Learning through ICT 126

Collaborative Learning and its Influences 130

Features Unique to E-Learning 130

Advantages of E-Learning to the Trainer or Organization 131

Advantages to the Learner 132

Disadvantages to the Trainer or Organization 132

Disadvantages to the Learner 133

Digital Story Telling 134

Combining Media to Tell a Story 137

Sources of Information and Learning 138

Framework for Learning Resources 138

Concept Mapping 139

Activity based Learning 141

References 142

CHAPTER 1

EDUCATIONAL TECHNOLOGY

Educational Technology (ET) is the efficient organization of any learning system adapting or adopting methods, processes, and products to serve identified educational goals. This involves systematic identification of the goals of education, recognition of the diversity of learners' needs, the contexts in which learning will take place, and the range of provisions needed for each of these. The challenge is to design appropriate systems that will provide for and enable appropriate teaching-learning systems that could realize the identified goals. The key to meeting this challenge is an appreciation of the role of ET as an agent of change in the classroom, which includes not only the teacher and the teaching-learning process but also systemic issues like reach, equity, and quality.

Over the past decades, educational technology in India has taken two routes. The first route involved a large number of experiments aimed at the qualitative improvement of schools, adopted the systems approach to analyze the problems plaguing the particular situation, and have evolved a range of solutions. These have included the development of flexible systems, alternative curricula, multilevel organization of classes; low-cost teaching-learning materials, innovative activities, continuous support systems for teacher training, etc. While many of these experiments have demonstrated intrinsic merit, they have been restricted to pockets of intense practice and have failed to influence the larger school system.

The second route is government sponsored schemes such as the Educational Technology (ET) Scheme and the Computer Literacy and Studies in Schools (CLASS) and their present-day analogues, including partnerships with global players. This included the supply of radio-cum-cassette players, colour televisions, micro-computers, present-day computer labs, and even satellite-receiving terminals. These schemes have largely remained supply-driven, equipment-centred, and disseminative in design. Scant attention has been paid to the development of the entire support system that would establish ET as a reliable, relevant, and timely intervention, and despite clear indications of the necessity for this action.

Information and Communication Technologies(ICTs) have brought in a convergence of the media along with the possibility of multi-centric participation in the content-generation and disseminative process. This has implications not only for the quality of the interchange but also for drastic upheavals of centre-dominated mindsets that have inhibited qualitative improvement. Modern ET has its potential in schools, in the teaching of subjects, in examinations, in research, in systemic reforms, and, above all, in teacher education, overcoming the conventional problems of scale and reach through online, anytime, anywhere. There exists today a well-established publishing industry, including desktop publishing, with know-how and capabilities in producing kits, teaching aids,etc.There also exist production capabilities for audio and video, multimedia, broadcast channels, Internet connectivity, trained manpower, and institutions with these mandates that can be leveraged to address the challenges of education.

Alternative models of education such as distance and open-learning, on-demand education, and other such flexible models of learning, will have to be tried and tested. Flexible systems, futuristic curricula, and a twenty-first-century career orientation have become a necessity for today's young people. There is an urgent need to convince the educational system, which should play an important role in engineering the teaching-learning situation and to make it a more meaningful experience for both teachers and their pupils.

Definition

Educational Technology could be defined in simple terms as the efficient organisation of any learning system, adapting or adopting methods, processes, and products to serve identified educational goals. It is the systematic identification of the goals of education, taking into account nationwide needs of higher scalability, the system capabilities, and the learners needs and potential.

Audio Visual Technology

Audio visual education or multimedia-based education is the instruction where particular attention is paid to the audio and visual presentation of the material with the goal of improving comprehension and retention. It also means possessing both a sound and a visual component, such as slide-tape presentations, films, television programs and live theatre productions. Business presentations are also often audio-visual. In a typical presentation, the presenter provides the audio by speaking and supplements it with a series of images projected onto a screen, either from a slide projector or from a computer connected to a projector using presentation software. Audio visual services providers frequently offer web streaming, video conferencing and live broadcast services. Computer based audio-visual equipment is often used in education, with many schools and universities installing projection equipment and using interactive white board technology.

Technology in Education

Electronic communication technology has become a fixture in many homes around the world, and its influence has permeated all facets of our lives, including educational settings.

Digital technologies are electronic tools, systems, devices and resources that generate store or process data:

- Social media
- Online games and applications
- Multimedia
- PowerPoint
- Productivity applications
- cloud computing
- Interoperable systems
- Mobile devices

It facilitate digital learning which is defined as any type of learning that is facilitate by technology or instructional practice that makes effective use of technology takes place across all learning areas and domains encompassing the application of a wide spectrum of practices including

- Blended and Virtual Learning
- Accessing Digital Content
- Local and Global collaboration, online reporting and assessment and using technology to connect, collaborate, curate and create.
- For teachers, ICTs provide a professional resource and mode of course delivery that takes advantage of all known learning modes, especially when combined with traditional face-to-face teaching.
- For students, ICTs provide opportunities to interact more effectively and to develop communicative and literacy skills

The most important benefits of using digital technologies reported by the students include:

- Improved academic skills (96.0%)
- Ability to make evaluative comments and contributions to the course (95.4%)
- Good source of learning from other relevant sites (90.0%)
- Making inferences from different topics (88.6%)
- Reorganising concepts, ideas, definitions and information on courses studied (87.7%), and
- Better understanding of the courses (87.0%)

Digital technologies are excellent aids for presentation to facilitate teaching and learning. It provided that each presentation is considered from an instructive, educational, academic/pedagogical viewpoint bearing in mind class size and different ways in which students learn to avoid passivity of students in classroom interaction. When used approximately and based on the creativity of user, power point is a flexible tool to improve and facilitate the development of interactive teaching and learning among faculty members and students.

Technology Evaluation in Education

Enhancing Education through Technology (EETT) program is part of the No Child Left Behind Act of 2001(NCLB) and, high-need school districts. The authorizing legislation specifically states three goals for the program:

a. To improve student academic achievement through the use of educational technology
b. To ensure that every student is technologically literate by the eighth grade and

c. To encourage the effective integration of technology in teacher training and curriculum development to establish research-based instructional methods that can be widely implemented as best practices.

Technology-Related Teacher Professional Development

Content of Technology-related Professional Development: More than two-thirds of studies reported providing technology-related professional development. Teachers in low- poverty schools were more likely to report receiving professional development that (a) introduced computers and the Internet (b) addressed how to use technology to enhance student learning in science and(c) taught how to use technology for grading.

Teacher-Reported Frequency of Professional Development: Overall, a more percentage of teachers had some form of technology-related professional development. Data reinforces that widespread availability of professional development that addresses how to use technology for grading. The next three most often cited topics for the technology-related professional development that teachers had received were the use of technology in developing curriculum and lesson plans, the use of technology to locate instructional materials on the Internet and the use of technology to support new teaching methods.

Needs of Teacher's High-poverty Schools: Teachers in high-poverty schools were consistently more likely than those in low-poverty schools to express a need for additional technology-related professional development. The biggest gap in needs between teachers in high-poverty schools and those in low-poverty schools was in the use of technology to meet the needs of language learners, teachers in high-poverty schools expressing a need for professional development in this area and a similar gap by school poverty level existed in teachers' perceived need for additional professional development in improving students' technology literacy.

Quality of Technology-related Professional Development: Seven characteristics often cited as elements of best practices for teacher professional development were identified through review of the literature (a) directly related to the content taught by the teacher, (b) included other members of the school community, (c) was consistent with the technology goals in the district, (d) provided an opportunity for meaningful engagement with colleagues and materials, (e) addressed different levels of teachers knowledge, skills and interest, (f) was delivered over multiple sessions, and (g) included follow-up activities (Means et al. 2004).

The most commonly reported feature of teachers self-described most useful professional development activity was directly related to the content taught. Teachers were least likely to report that their most useful professional development activity included follow-up activities.

Percentage of Teachers Meeting Technology Standards: One of the GPRA measures for the EETT program is the percentage of teachers who meet their state technology standards. Only few states have minimum technology competency standards for teachers and states were generally not collecting data regarding the GPRA measure of the percentage of teachers meeting state technology standards. Among them the definitions and measurement of teachers' technology competency varied greatly.

However, the data are not normally distributed, and the modal district response suggests that a high proportion of teachers in particular districts met district standards. About two out of every five districts that reported a percentage of teachers indicated that 91 percent to 100 percent of teachers met district technology standards.

Integration of Technology into Teaching and Learning

District Wide Integration of Technology: The GPRA measure for technology integration is the percentage of areas receiving Educational Technology State Grants funds[EETT funds] that have effectively and fully integrated technology. However, as reported by the state survey, most states either had not adopted a definition of effective integration of technology or did not measure the percentage of districts meeting the statewide definition.

Teacher and Student Use of Technology for Teaching and Learning: Larger percentages of teachers reported using technology for a variety of professional practices on a weekly basis. The biggest gains were in teacher's use of technology to develop curricula or assignments in reading, math, or other subjects and to present reading, math, or other subject concepts to students. The only two exceptions to this trend were using technology to test students, which decreased, and using technology to collaborate with experts or teachers in other locations. During the same time frame, the frequency of student's use of technology for schoolwork, as reported by teachers, did not change. The only significant difference between the two years was an increase in the use of technology to prepare for standardized tests.

Student Technology Literacy

Assessing Student Technology Literacy: One of the GPRA measures for the EETT program is the percentage of students who meet state technology standards by the end of the eighth grade. Either stand-alone technology standards for students or technology standards that were integrated into other student academic standards. The average percentage of students meeting technology literacy standards was 64 percent. Small number of states assessing student technology literacy and the very different assessment approaches and grade levels tested, aggregated state-reported student proficiency rates must be viewed with particular caution. The Enhancing Education through Technology (EETT) program is the most comprehensive program that supports improving student academic achievement in elementary and secondary schools through the use of educational technology. The EETT program also seeks:

- To ensure that every student is technologically literate by the time he or she finishes the eighth grade, regardless of the student's race, ethnicity, gender, family income, geographic location or disability, and
- To encourage the effective integration of technology resources and systems with teacher training and curriculum development to establish research-based instructional methods that can be widely implemented as best practices.

AVRC

The Educational Multimedia Research Centre (EMMRC) was established as Audio Visual Research Centre (AVRC) by the UGC-CEC under the Country-Wide Classroom (CWC) Project with the following objectives.

- Production of educational programmes(especially video and audio)and related support material and setting up of appropriate facilities for this.
- Research related to optimizing the effectiveness of the programmes.
- Providing a forum for the active involvement of academic and other scholars in the creation of appropriate educational programme.
- Studying, promoting and experimenting with new techniques/ technology that will increase the reach and/or effectiveness of educational communication.

The Centre is presently funded by the UGC and MHRD for producing enrichment, educational video lecture and e-content programmes for broadcasting these through educational channel on Doordarshan and Internet streaming commanding a viewership of more than 25 million students.

The Centre is equipped with a large state-of-the-art studio with chroma facility, latest technology broadcasting equipment and high-powered multimedia workstations to produce educational video content, LORs and e-content programmes. Besides this, the Centre also conducts research related to the creation, dissemination and evaluation of educational content.

EMMRC

In 1984 University Grants Commission (UGC), New Delhi has launched Countrywide Class Room (CWCR) and production facilities at 6 universities in India through establishing media centres in the name of Audio Visual Research Centres (AVRCs) later these centres have been renamed as Educational Multimedia Research Centres (EMMRCS). This was mainly to use electronic media for the quality enrichment of higher education AUGC began its transmission of Country Wide Class Room (CWCR) programme from 15th August 1984. Through Doordarshan National network, initially the co-ordination with these centres was done from UGC office with the support of a consultant. Subsequently, an Inter-University Centre named as Consortium for Educational Communication'(CEC) was set up in the year 1993 to co-ordinate with media centres (AVRCs and EMMRCs) and to make CWCR mission most effective and successful.The Educational Multimedia Research Centre(EMMRC) was established as Audio Visual Research Centre (AVRC) by the UGC-CEC under the Country-Wide Classroom(CWC) Project, with the following objectives.

- Production of educational programmes(especially video and audio)and related support material and setting up of appropriate facilities for this.
- Research related to optimizing the effectiveness of the programmes.
- Providing a forum for the active involvement of academic and other scholars in the creation of appropriate educational programme.
- Studying,promoting and experimenting with new techniques/technology that will increase the reach and/or effectiveness of educational communication.

The Centre is presently funded by the UGC and MHRD for producing enrichment educational video lecture and e-content programmes for broadcasting these through educational channels. The Centres are equipped with a large state-of-the-art studio with chroma facility, latest technology broadcasting equipment and high-powered multimedia workstations to produce educational video content LORs and e-content programmes.

EDUSAT

In the year 2004 the Govt. of India launched a dedicated Satellite called EDUSAT (Educational Satellite) to serve the educational sectors offering an interactive satellite based distance education system for the country. It is to provide connectivity to schools, colleges, and other similar institutions. Initially it is proposed to use the facilities in four different states for reaching different target groups Karnataka, Kerala, Madhya Pradesh and Maharastra are the four States where EDUSAT programme are implemented in the current year. In each of these States a particular target and area has been identified for utilization of EDUSAT). Different agencies have been identified in for implementing the EDUSAT Project. The State council of Educational Research and Training is entrusted with the responsibility for the development of Software, Teacher Training, Monitoring & Evaluation and overall implementation of the project. Indian Space Research Organisation**(ISRO)**, Serva Siksha Abhiyan**(SSA)** are also involved in the implementation the Programme. Each of these agencies was entrusted with certain tasks for facilitating the implementation.

Countrywide Classrooms

The present decade is witnessing chaotic and seemingly unplanned developments in the educational television scenario in India. Countrywide Classroom, which ran on the National Network of Doordarshan for almost over 20 years, has been taken off the air. Instead, we have three channels dedicated to higher education-Gyan Darshan run by IGNOU, the technology channel Eklavya and Vyasa channel-the new avatar of Countrywide Classroom run by CEC. Programmes are being produced for these channels with public funds. Most of these programmes are presumably significant in terms of their content and production value. However, all the three channels have very poor visibility and so the programmes go, by and large, unwatched. The entire exercise of production of educational television programmes seems to be a wasteful exercise. The research charts the development of 'Countrywide Classroom' over the past 40 years and suggests viable models for some of its future activities.

The Advantages and Disadvantages of Using ICT for Teaching and Learning

Many of the Internet projects require students to communicate with students from different states or countries via electronic mail or mailing lists or other news groups. Furthermore, The Internet should be a part of an integrated teaching system. It should be seen as a tool that supports and enhances learning and not as a means by itself. Teaching using the Internet does not by itself lead to achieving curriculum objectives, because part nom assisting in class preparation, a good knowledge of the Internet allows us to assist our students in their class activities involving the Internet. Besides,

Professional Development is a key to updating skills and for career advancement for teachers. Among others, we can use the Internet to join a discussion group, subscribe to a news group, take classes, and keep in touch with professional colleagues. To successfully use the Internet for teaching, we must know how to access the various services available through the Internet. Moreover, it has been reported that the majority of teachers who use the Internet in teaching are those who believe that the Internet is a new way for doing things. These teachers also use the Internet for shopping, banking, looking for mortgage rates, etc. They emphasize teacher training as a key to effective use of computer technology in the classroom. Every new technology brings with it positive and negative impact. Nobody has taken time to analyze the negative impact of exposing students to the Internet may have on their social development.

How the Internet Enhances the Teaching Process

Using the Internet to add value, manage our classroom or improve the planning. To teach using the internet because we want to change, improve, add a new dimension to our teaching, or vary the types and increase the quality of activities assigned to students. In learning, the students need some motivation. Allow them to use the Internet in their learning is a motivational push to who are bored by the traditional ways of information delivery, and thereby expedite the transfer of information from the short-term memory to the long-term memory. The Internet allows us to motivate some of the lost students in the class, and thereby accelerate the assimilation process.

Communication is a way of using knowledge. It is a source for re-enforcement. The Internet promotes fast communication across geographical barriers, and therefore gives students an opportunity to communicate early in life with a broad range of people not imagined possible before. Also using knowledge in different settings give a better understanding of the different shades of meaning of the concepts involved in a giving learning situation.

The Internet allows you to add content to your lessons and to disseminate useful information to students and parents without waste of valuable class time and those give many advantages for students in learning. Flexibility supports collaborative learning among students who can therefore participate at times and places of their choosing. States that student may participate at any time of the day or night that they have the time and the inclination. Opportunities for feedback from the instructor and interaction with other students are not limited to a few fixed times per week.

Advantages of Students Using ICT for Learning

As it was pointed out previously, internet provides students with the tools they need to discover and own knowledge. And give students the hooks and templates they need to fasten information to the long-term memory. There are some advantages of student using ICT for learning.

Motivating Factor

The Internet can act as a motivating tool for many students. Young people are very captivated with technology. Educators must capitalize on this interest, excitement, and enthusiasm about the Internet for the purpose of enhancing learning. For already enthusiastic learners, the Internet allows you to provide them with additional learning activities not readily available in the classroom.

Fast Communication

The Internet promotes fast communication across geographical barriers. Your students can join collaborative projects that involve students from different states, countries or continents. This type of learning experience was not possible before the Internet. This is a unique learning experience very essential for each of our students, as the world is becoming one big community.

Cooperative Learning

The Internet facilitates co-operative learning, encourages dialogue and creates a more engaging classroom. For example, our class will allow your students to get involved in class discussions through e-mails in a way not possible within the four walls of the classroom.

Locating Research Materials

Apart from communication, research is what takes many people to the Internet. There are many more resources on the Internet than the school library can provide. We can encourage students to take advantage of this wealth of resources on the Internet for their research.

Acquiring Varied Writing Skills

Students require publishing their work on the internet, they have to develop hypertext skills, if these skills help students gain experience in non-sequential writings. Moreover and since the Internet is open to all with access, students publishing their work on the Internet are forced to be mindful of their language and to write to non-expert audience.

Disadvantages of Using ICT for Education

The use of the Internet for education is not without problems. Therefore, one should expect the problems to be encountered in using the Internet in teaching to be evolving as well. There are some disadvantage of using ICT for teaching and learning.

Plagiarism

Apart from Web sites that claim to help students write term papers, there are numerous cases of students downloading information from the Net and turning them in for grades. We can minimize this problem by requiring students to cite research sources. This can assist us in minimizing cases of plagiarism in the class. This service claims to prevent plagiarism by determining if a term paper has been copied from the Internet or not.

Student Privacy

Criminals, marketers, and other persons can easily get information from students when they are online. These could post danger to student's lives or may even lead to litigation against the school. To avoid this problem, students should be educated on the dangers of giving information to people online. Parents and teachers need to supervise students' online activities.

Low Income Groups

Over 50% of public schools with a high minority enrollment had a lower rate of internet access than the public schools with a low minority enrollment. The same was true of instructional rooms in those schools. In addition, students from low-income families may not have computers at home or may have computers at home with no access to the Internet. Consequently, students in low-income communities may be disadvantaged.

To reduce the effect that social or economic status may have, we should give Internet assignments that students can easily complete while in school. If necessary, schools may need to keep computer labs open for longer and/or odd hours. The use of computers at public libraries should also be encouraged.

Preparation Time

It takes a lot of preparation time to effectively use the net for education. In addition to designing Internet based lesson plans, we may have to surf the Internet to download lesson plans and adapt them to support the curriculum objectives or visit sites to select those appropriate for classes. We have no choice but prepare in order to help your students become responsible user of the Internet. Teaching using the internet brings to bear a new set of administrative demands on the teacher and the school administration. These include development and implementation of acceptable use policy, training, developing new evaluation criteria as needed, and addressing parents' concerns.

E-learning

The Internet has become one of the vital ways to make available resources for research and learning for both teachers and students to share and acquire information Technology-based e-learning encompasses the use of the internet and other important technologies to produce materials for learning, teach learners, and also regulate courses in an organization. There has been extensive debate about a common definition of the term e-learning. Existing definitions according to (Dublin, 2003) tend to reveal the specialization and interest of the researchers. E-learning as a concept covers a range of applications, learning methods and processes (Rossi, 2009).

E-Learning has transformed from a fully-online course to using technology to deliver part or all of a course independent of permanent time and place. The use of new multimedia technologies and the Internet to increase learning quality by easing access to facilities and services as well as distant exchanges and collaboration. The following are also different definitions of e-learning. The use of information and communication technologies to enable the access to online learning/teaching resources. E–learning is defined as the use of information and communication technologies in diverse processes of education to support and enhance learning in institutions of higher education, and includes the usage of information and communication technology as a complement to traditional classrooms, online learning or mixing the two modes.

Advantages

The adoption of E-learning in education, especially for higher educational institutions has several benefits, and given its several advantages and benefits, e-learning is considered among the best methods of education.

- The adoption of e-learning provides the institutions as well as their students or learners the much flexibility of time and place of delivery or receipt of according to learning information.
- E-learning enhances the efficacy of knowledge and qualifications via ease of access to a huge amount of information.
- It is able to provide opportunities for relations between learners by the use of discussion forums. Through this, e-learning helps eliminate barriers that have the potential of hindering participation including the fear of talking to other learners.
- E-learning motivates students to interact with other, as well as exchange and respect different point of views.

- E-learning is cost effective in the sense that there is no need for the students or learners to travel. It is also cost effective in the sense that it offers opportunities for learning for maximum number of learners with no need for many buildings.

- E-learning always takes into consideration the individual learners differences. Some learners, for instance prefer to concentrate on certain parts of the course, while others are prepared to review the entire course.

- E-learning helps compensate for scarcities of academic staff, including instructors or teachers as well as facilitators, lab technicians etc.

- The use of e-Learning allows self-pacing. For instance the asynchronous way permits each student to study at his or her own pace and speed whether slow or quick.

Disadvantages

- E-learning as a method of education makes the learners undergo contemplation, remoteness, as well as lack of interaction or relation. It therefore requires a very strong inspiration as well as skills with to the management of time in order to reduce such effects.

- E-learning method might be less effective that the traditional method of learning. The learning process is much easier with the use of the face to face encounter with the instructors or teachers.

- When it comes to improvement in communication skills of learners, e-learning as a method might have a negative effect. The learners though have an excellent knowledge in academics, they may not possess the needed skills to deliver their acquired knowledge to others.

- E-learning are possibly done with the use of proxy, it will be difficult, if not impossible to control or regulate bad activities like cheating.

- E-learning may also probably be misled to piracy and plagiarism, predisposed by inadequate selection skills, as well as the ease of copy and pasted.

- Researchers have argued that e-learning is more appropriate in social science and humanities than the fields such as medical science and pharmacy, where there is the need to develop practical skills.

- E-learning may also lead to congestion or heavy use of some websites. This may bring about unanticipated costs both in time and money.

Open Educational Resources

Since its establishment in 1985 by an act of parliament, the Indira Gandhi National Open University (IGNOU) has contributed significantly to the development of higher education in India through the open and distance learning (ODL) mode. It was established with a vision to serve as a national resource centre for ODL, with international recognition and presence, to provide seamless access for all too sustainable and learner-centric quality education, skills upgrading and training, using innovative technologies and methodologies. IGNOU has emerged as the largest university in the democratic world, serving the educational aspirations of around 2.8 million students in India and 32 other countries. IGNOU's learning resource repository, e-GyanKosh, initiated in 2005 with the intention of digitizing self-instructional material, has emerged as one of the world's largest repositories, with more than 40,000 self-instructional text materials, and around 2,000 video-lectures covering over 2,200 of the university's courses. The repository has become very popular in a short time and is being used the world over by student and teacher communities for its rich content. So far, the courses available on e-GyanKosh and Flexi Learn have been licensed material available as open access content that one can register to use free of cost, but that is non-derivative, non-reusable and governed by copyright rules.

The university has now decided to provide all its learning resources as Open Educational Resources(OER) through its open licence policy. IGNOU envisions that it will be a leading developer of OER, with the use of its own as well as others' OER fully incorporated into teaching and learning at all levels within the university system. This case study provides an insight into the process of e-GyanKosh evolving from a digital repository to an OER repository.

1. International jurisdiction, taking IGNOU programmes Asian countries, including Maldives, Mauritius, Nepal and Seychelles, covering in all 43 countries.
2. Flexible admission rules.
3. Individualized study with flexibility in terms of place, pace and duration.
4. Use of state-of-the-art information and communication technology(ICT) applications.
5. A student support service network in the country, as well as at the international level through partner institutions.
6. Resource sharing, collaboration and networking with conventional universities and other organizations.
7. Socially and academically relevant programmes based on needs assessments.
8. Special education catering to underserved populations and the disadvantaged.

Important Achievements

- Emergence as the largest university in the world.
- Recognition as a Centre of Excellence in Distance Education by the Commonwealth of Learning in 199.
- Award of Excellence for Distance Education Materials by the Commonwealth of Learning in 1999.

- Listed 12th in the Webometrics ranking of Indian universities in January 2010.

IGNOU provides multi-channel, multiple media teaching and learning packages m the form of self-instructional print and audio/video materials, radio and television broadcasts, face-to- face counselling/tutoring, laboratory and hands-on experience, videoconferencing, interactive radio counselling, interactive multimedia CD/DVD and Internet-based learning. Apart from the print-based self-instructional material, the educational programmes reach more than ten million homes through Gyan Darshan TV channels, a DTH (direct-to-home) platform, Gyan Vani radio stations and webcasting. The Electronic Media Production Centre (EMPC) of the university has emerged as a major hub for the nation in using electronic media in distance education.

Web-based programmes and information systems that provide access to users who are physically remote from resources is emerging as a democratizing, emancipating, empowering force, facilitating self-publishing, knowledge sharing and peer-to-peer networking. The Internet has now evolved from being a medium in which information was transmitted and consumed, into a platform where content is created, shared, remixed, repurposed and redistributed. In the same spirit, eLearning has moved from being merely a content repository, emulating classroom teaching, to more dynamic concepts of social networking, do-it-yourself, personal learning environments and mobile learning. Realizing the potential of online learning to reach out to the unreached, IGNOU has embarked on major initiatives towards developing online learning environments for distance learners.

History of the Internet

Internet use in high education institutions as a teaching and learning tool implies large-scale involvement from all the areas of an academic community: institution management, professors, students and staff. Importance of the institutional strategy that reflects the diversity of ways ICTs may be used in different context across the institution.

The development of technology, particularly of the technologies regarding the information transfer and communication are important elements to ensure the companies competitiveness. In respect with all above-mentioned points of view, we conclude that the academic curriculum has to include deeper IT&C components and help accounting students acquire specific competences.

E-learning allows students with limited mobility or inflexible schedules to take courses and study at times that are convenient for them using Internet aiming to gather information.

- Share the information retrieved on Internet with the students aiming at engaging them in additional learning activities
- Students are working on the Internet as part of the lesson plan
- The curriculum prepared by the teacher includes projects and activities that can be accomplished just by using the Internet
- Students are designing their projects based on Internet activities, following a self-directed learning.

Internet and Education

The Internet is registering a huge and rapid growth, and this growth is expected to continue at significant rates at a global scale. The expansion is explained by the tremendous impact of the Internet on the economic, financial, social, political systems as well as at the individuals' level. Practically, the Internet has become part of billions of peoples' daily life.

The Internet expansion has potentiated business globalization, the communication channels use-by the huge numbers of users, very divers in their type and communication scope, the information society construct in many states and various other social and individuals' aspects. Internet is a world in a continuous expansion and change. The change of the companies' perception over the external factors influence reveals that globalization has been understood, in time, as a normal process and the internet user's skills have become natural for many people. Starting from the students preferences on Internet use, the quality of the electronic source citations used by the students in their studies.

The Internet provides rapid and easy access to the information of all kind, and as a result has become an important search information tool for the students. "Surfing on Internet for course material has positive net effect on intellectual development and vocational preparation, in addition to personal development. Students acquire the useful skills to perform a critically information search on Internet. In this respect, (Gaytan, 2000) recommends that students internet-based learning experiences have to be developed by their teachers. Internet use in high education institutions as a teaching and learning tool implies large-scale involvement from all the areas of an academic community institution management, professors, students and staff. Importance of the institutional strategy that reflects the diversity of ways ICTs may be used in different context across the institution.

The exponential development of the Internet has impacted the socio-economical, political life and individuals' life and will continue to significantly impact the society in all its aspects. Internet has changed the business environment, the socio-political domains and peoples' behavior and cultural values. In this context, the authors surveys aimed at identify and understand the internet user's profile of the students in one of the Romanian faculty.

The survey revealed the students' Internet use and time spending on Internet. The research emphasized that the survey's respondents could be considered extensive Internet users for personal needs and less effective users for professional purposes. The study's findings provided important insights regarding Internet access and use preferences of our students and emphasized how the teaching process can exploit, in an effective way, the students' skills and appetite for Internet use. The findings pointed out the needed updates in the academic curriculum aiming at providing skills and knowledge in regard with Internet effective use for learning and professional purposes.

The Internet is a powerful tool for assisting students and educators with conducting research. Going to a library and searching through a card catalog by hand can be laborious and inefficient compared to searching for the same information on a computer. One of the most powerful benefits of the Internet in higher education is its role in e-Learning, E-Learning uses course materials that exist entirely on a computer or the Internet. Some schools offer courses that are entirely e-learning based, meaning all texts, assignments, quizzes and tests are accessible online and no face-to-face meetings are required.

Critical Issues in Internet Usages

The Internet has revolutionized the computer and communications world like nothing before. The invention of the telegraph, telephone, radio, and computer set the stage for this unprecedented integration of capabilities. The Internet is at once a world-wide broadcasting capability, a mechanism for information dissemination, and a medium for collaboration and interaction between individuals and their computers without regard for geographic location. The Internet represents one of the most successful examples of the benefits of sustained investment and commitment to research and development of information infrastructure. Beginning with the early research in packet switching, the government, industry and academia have been partners in evolving and deploying this exciting new technology.

The Internet today is a widespread information infrastructure, the initial prototype 01 what is often called the national infrastructure. Its history is complex and involves many aspects-technological, organizational, and community. And its influence reaches not only to the technical fields of computer communications but throughout society as we move toward increasing use of online tools to accomplish electronic commerce, information acquisition, and community operations.

- Internet is a most powerful educational tool for teaching Learning.
- Internet is useful for self-study to student.
- Internet gives to student a lot of information for student to achieve goal.
- Internet could also be used for assignment and the progress of student.

Origins of the Internet

The first recorded description of the social interactions that could be enabled through networking was aeries of memos written by J.C.R. Likelier, 1962 of MIT in August 1962 discussing his galactic network concept. He envisioned a globally interconnected set of computer's through which everyone could quickly access defend programs from any site. In spirit, the concept was very much like the internet of today. Likelier was the first head of the computer research program at DARPA, starting in October 1962.In October 1972, Kahn organized a large, very successful demonstration of the ARPANET at the International Computer Communication Conference (ICCC). This was the first public demonstration of this new network technology to the public. It was also in 1972 that the initial hot application, electronic mail, was introduced. In March Ray Tomlinson at BBN wrote the basic email message send and read software, motivated by the need of the ARPANET developers for an easy coordination mechanism. In July, Roberts expanded its utility by writing the first email utility program to list, selectively read, file, forward, and respond to messages. From there email took off as the largest network application for over a decade. This was a harbinger of the kind of activity we see on the World Wide Web today, namely, the enormous growth of all kinds of people-to-people traffic.

Web Browser

A web browser is a software application for retrieving, presenting, and traversing information resources on the World Wide Web. An information resource is identified by a Uniform Resource Identifier (URI/URL) and may be a web page, image, video or other piece of content hyperlinks present in resources enable users easily to navigate their browsers to related resources. Although browsers are primarily intended to use the World Wide Web, they can also be used to access information provided by web servers in private networks or files in file systems. The major web browsers are Firefox, Internet Explorer/Microsoft Edge, Google Chrome, Opera, and Safari. The first web browser was invented in 1990 by Sir Tim Berners- Lee. Berners-Lee is the director of the World Wide Web Consortium (W3C), which oversees the Web's continued development, and is also the founder of the World Wide Web Foundation. His browser was called Worldwide Web and later renamed Nexus. The first commonly available web browser with a graphical user interface was Erwise. The development of Erwise was initiated by Robert Cailliau. The most recent major entrant to the browser market is Chrome, first released in September 2008. Chrome's take-up has increased significantly year by year, by doubling its usage share from 8% to 16% by August 2011. This increase seems largely to be at the expense of Internet Explorer, whose share has tended to decrease from month to month. In December 2011, Chrome overtook Internet

Explorer 8 as the most widely used web browser but still had lower usage than all versions of Internet Explorer combined.

Function

The primary purpose of a web browser is to bring information resources to the user allowing them to view the information and then access other information. This process begins when the user inputs a Uniform Resource Locator (URL), for example http://en.wikipedia.org/, into the browser. The prefix of the URL, the Uniform Resource Identifier or URI, determines how the URL will be interpreted. HTML and associated content (image files, formatting information such as CSS, etc.,) is passed to the browser's layout engine to be transformed from markup to an interactive document, a process known as "rendering". Information resources may contain hyperlinks to other information resources. Each link contains the URI of a resource to go to. When a link is clicked, the browser navigates to the resource indicated by the link's target URI, and the process of bringing content to the user begins again.

User Interface

Back and forward buttons to go back to the previous resource and forward respectively.

- A refresh or reload button to reload the current resource.
- A stop button to cancel loading the resource.
- An address bar to input the Uniform Resource Identifier (URI) of the desired resource and display it.
- A status bar to display progress in loading the resource also the URI of links when the cursor hovers over them, and page zooming capability.
- The viewport, the visible area of the webpage within the browser window. The ability to view the HTML source for a page.

CHAPTER 2

COMMUNICATION TECHNOLOGY IN EDUCATION

Derived from the Greek word "communicare" or "communico" which means "to share". In 21st century, the communication technology becomes more developed in this world. It is acting an important role in our daily life. It could help us to communicate with others, sharing our information. Communication technology could also help us to finish our work very fast and efficiently. It brings us many advantages in our social life. It could help us to communicate our families, friends, and our other relatives. For examples: Tango, Skype and others. We could immediately voice call them, text them, or even video call them. We could know what they done recently and we could see each other through video calls. It is useful and convenient for the teenagers, students, and businessman. It could help them to search information within a short time. For businessman, they could save money and time by doing their transaction through video call.

For poor family, they could just connect the wi-fi that provided to contact the others through many apps such as Wechat, Line, Whatsapp and others. They could contact other without spending any money and they could just use a few minutes and even just a few second to post their pictures and check-in on facebook to lets the others know their recently places. For the people who like to read news, they could search the recently news faster than those who buy newspaper. They would also gets to know more information compared to the others who not using internet.

Concept

Communication is an elusive concept and is difficult to arrive at a precise definition. Communication is so deeply rooted in human behaviors and the structures of society that it is difficult to think of society without communication. We may say that communication literally means transmitting information from one person to another. But many scholars of communication take this as a working definition. In reality sometimes communication refers to some human acts, it may refer to discipline of knowledge as well; it also refers to some kind of process as well.

Characteristics and Elements

While defining the communication we should keep in mind that the definition of the term "Communication" is not uniform and it varies in point of reference to the context. To understand communication as a process we suppose communication consists of different mechanisms/phenomenon made up of different elements interrelated in a particular way for giving certain output. These elements together form a process. These elements are:

1. Source/Sender
2. Encoding
3. Message
4. Channel
5. Decoding
6. Receiver
7. Feedback
8. Noise
9. Context

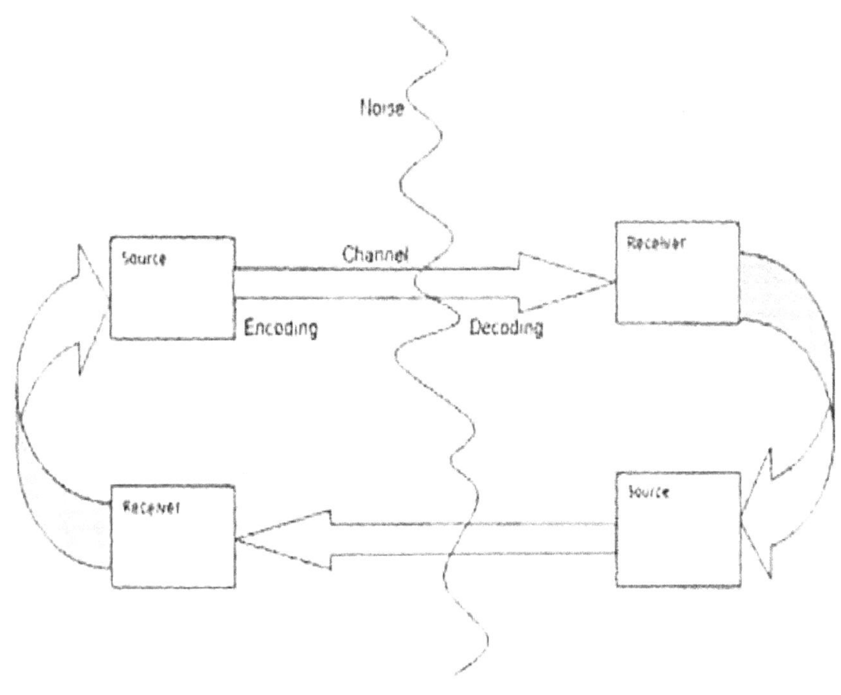

Elements of Communication

Sender

The communicator or sender is the person or group who is sending the message. The sender starts the process of communication.

Encoding

Encoding means the translation of the messages to the form which can be understood by the receiver. The Messages are generally encoded in the forms of codes. These codes may be Languages or nonverbal commands.

Message

Message the coded information which, sender is trying to send to the receiver. It is the most important element of the communication process as it is the thing to be conveyed.

Channel

Channel is the pathway along which our message is carried. It's the medium. For example air while transmitting voices, telephone wire etc.,

Decoding

Decoding is the opposite of in coding process. It reverses the code to get the exact information. The decoder could be a machine or a person and the ability of the decoder affects the process. For example, a blind man cannot get the information through reading a written message. The change in meaning between the encoder and the decoder is known as aberrant decoding.

Receiver

For whom the message is targeted is the receiver. After the message is decoded the Lesage is perceived or understood by the receiver. The main purpose of the communication process is to provide receiver the information. A receiver could be a person or an institution.

Feedback

The response of the receiver after receiving the message is the feedback. It represents the reversal of the flow of the communication. There are two types of feedback. They are: positive feedback and negative feedback.

Noise

Anything that interferes or blocks the original path of a message is known as noise. It provides negative catalysm to the communication process. There is no such thing as perfect communication. Noise could be of three types: Semantic noise, mechanical noise, and environmental noise.

Semantic noise is the blockage in communication when people have different meaning for different words and phrases. Mechanical noise is the noise produced by the malfunctioning of the machine which is used for communication and environmental noises are those which are produced by the external factors.

Context

Context is the situation of the surrounding where the communication is taking place. It could be the sociocultural, political, economic or even pschycological situation. Context affects the communication process directly.

Characteristics of Communication

Some of the characteristics of communication are discussed below:

- Communication is a process.
- There are senders and receivers in his process.
- Communication is transactional.
- Communication is symbolic.
- The quality of a communication process depends upon participants as well as the channel Involved.
- Success or failure depends both on sender and receiver.
- Information is shared in the process.
- It is closely associated with culture.

Essentials of Communication Process

Communication process always needs a medium, and beyond this, these things are essential for the effective communication.

- A common communication environment.
- Mutual cooperation between sender and receiver.
- Appropriate channel.
- Correct encoding and decoding of the message.
- Response and feedback.

Types of Communication

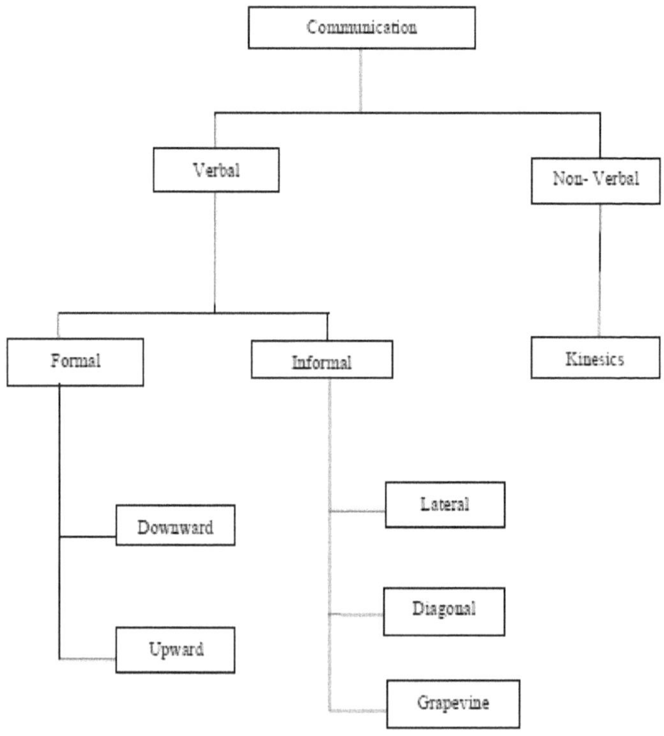

Verbal Communication

Two types of verbal communication

- Formal communication
- Informal communication

Formal Communication

- We use this type of communication in offices and social gathering.
- Two types of formal communication.

  (1) Downward

  (2) Upward

Downward Communication

- Higher designation to lower designation
- Ex. Boss ordered his worker.
- Here effect of this type of communication is very much than upward communication

Upward Communication

- Lower designation to higher designation.
- Ex. Worker request to his boss.
- Here the effect of communication is less than downward communication.

Informal Communication

- We use this type of communication with our family or friends.
- Three types of informal communication.

  1. Lateral

  2. Diagonal

  3. Grapevine

Lateral Communication

- Found among members working at the same level.
- Ex-peer group.
- Most effective form of communication.
- Barrier of subordinates or boss is not present here.

Diagonal Communication

- The path is mixture of vertical and horizontal movement.
- In large communications various departments need communication support from each other.

Grapevine Communication

- Also called as "backbiting" or "backstabbing".
- A backstabber is a colleague or an employee who acts like a friend in public but badmouth you in private.

Non-verbal Communication

- Through signs & symbols
- Non-verbal can go without verbal communication
- Verbal can't go without non-verbal communication

Models of Communication

- Simplest model of communication reflects the work of Shannon and Weaver.
- Model consists of a sender, a message, a channel where the message travels, noise or interference and a receiver.
- Often, communicator's blame the audience for not accepting a message, but it is often that the sender, encoding process or channels chosen were not applied correctly.

- First model is missing an essential step in the communications process-feedback.
- Without feedback, we don't know if the receiver received or understood our message.
- Design and deliver message so that it gets the attention of intended audience.
- Relate to common experiences between the source and destination.
- Offer a way to meet personality needs appropriate to the group situation the receiver is in at the time you want that receiver to respond.

Wilbur Schramm

- Communication is something people do.
- There is no meaning in a message except what people put into it.
- To understand human communication process, one must understand how people relate to each other.

Wilbur Schramm's Modifications

- Added to the model the context of the relationship, and how that relationship will affect Communicator A and Communicator B.
- Included the social environment in the model, noting that it will influence the frame of reference of both Communicator A and B.

The Seven Cs of Communication help Overcome Barriers

1. Clarity
2. Credibility
3. Content
4. Context
5. Continuity
6. Capability
7. Channels

Types of Classroom Communication

Classroom communication exists in three categories: verbal, nonverbal and written. Verbal communication means anything that a teacher or student speaks aloud. Nonverbal communication refers to body language that people express. Written communication is writing directed at a specific audience, such as report card comments or student assignments. Teachers and students interact with one another in many different contexts, and use all three of these types of communication.

Teacher/Class Communication

Teacher/class communication exists when a teacher communicates with his entire class. Verbal communication exists when a teacher tells students information they need to know. There are ways for teachers to communicate nonverbally with their classes, such as through their posture, gesticulations and proximity to the students. Instead of telling a student to stop talking, a teacher could use nonverbal communication by moving toward the disruptive student's desk. Not only does the disruptive student receive the message, but other students in the class who observe the intervention receive it as well. Written instructions for an assignment are given from the teacher for the whole class.

Teacher /Student Communication

It occurs when a teacher interacts directly with a particular student. Since a teacher interacts with her student mostly in front of the whole class. It can be difficult to distinguish teacher/student communication from teacher/class communication. Teacher/student communication requires that the teacher act one-on-one with a student, such as in a conference during class activities, before or after class or after school.

This type of communication is effective for teacher who wants to communicate a private message, such as a talk about constant inappropriate behavior or about taking more of a leadership role in class.

Student /Teacher Communication

It is also direct communication between a student and the teacher, but this time is the student who initiates the conversation. Also, this can occur during whole-class participation. The reason the reverse situation constitutes teacher/class communication and not teacher/student is that the teacher's actions and message are directed toward the whole class while the student's questions here are only directed at the teacher. When students write emails to their teacher on graded assignments, this constitutes a written form of student/teacher communication.

Communication Network

Communication network is the infrastructure that allows two or more computers(called hosts) to communicate with each other. The network achieves this by providing a set of rules for communication, called protocols, which should be observed by all participating hosts. The need for a protocol should be obvious: It allows different computers from different vendors and with different operating characteristics to 'speak the same language'.

Network Components

The network is made up of two types of components: nodes and communication lines. The nodes typically handle the network protocols and provide switching capabilities. A node is usually itself a computer (general or special) which runs specific network software. The communication lines may take many different shapes and forms, even in the same network. Examples include copper wire cables, optical fiber, radio channels, and telephone lines. A host is connected to the network by a separate communication line which connects it to one of the nodes. In most cases, more than one host may be connected to the same node. From a host's point of view, the entire network may be viewed as a black box, to which many other hosts are connected. Each host has a unique address allocated to it by the network. For a host to communicate with another host, it needs to know the latter's address. All communication between hosts passes through the nodes, which in turn determine how to route messages across the network, from one point to another.

Network Types

The OSI Model

The International Standards Organization (ISO) has developed a reference model for network design called the Open Systems Interconnection (OSI). It proposes seven-layer architecture for networks. Each layer is characterized by set of standard protocols which specify its behavior.

The Physical Layer

The physical layer is concerned with the transmission of raw data bits over communication lines. Physical layer standards and protocols are concerned with issues such as the following:

- How a physical circuit is established between communicating devices.
- How the circuit is terminated when no longer needed.
- The physical form (e.g., voltages, frequencies and timing) in which data bits (binary values 0 and 1) are represented.
- Whether transmission of data can take place in one or both directions over the same physical connection.
- Characteristics of the physical media that carry the signals (e.g., copper wire, optical fiber, radio waves).

- Characteristics of the connectors used for connecting the physical media.

- How data from a number of sources should be multiplexed before transmission and demultiplexed upon arrival, and the type of multiplexing technique to be used.

- The type of modulation to be used for transmitting digital data over analog transmission lines.

The physical layer accounts for much of the tangible components of a network, including cables, satellites, earth stations, repeaters, multiplexers, concentrators, and modems. Physical layer protocols and standards are of mechanical, electrical, functional, and procedural nature. The physical layer hides the above details from the higher layers. To the data link layer, it appears as a logical communication channel which can send a stream of bits from one point in the network to another (but not necessarily reliably).

The Data Link Layer

The data link layer is concerned with the reliable transfer of data over the communication channel provided by the physical layer. To do this, the data link layer breaks the data into data frames, transmits the frames sequentially over the channel, and checks for transmission errors by requiring the receiving end to send back acknowledgment frames. Data link protocols are concerned with the following issues:

- How to divide the data into frames.

- How to delimit frames by adding special bit patterns to the beginning and end of each frame. This allows the receiving end to detect where each frame begins and where it ends.

- **Error Detection**: Some form of error check is included in the frame header. This is constructed by the transmitting end based on the contents of the frame, and checked for integrity by the receiving end. A change in the frame bits can be detected in this way.

- **Error Correction**: When a frame arrives corrupted or is for any reason lost in the network, it is retransmitted. Lost acknowledgment frames may result in duplicate frames, which need to be detected and corrected as well.

- **Flow Control**: In general, not all communication devices in a network operate at the same speed. Flow control provides a means of avoiding a slow receiver from being swamped by data from a fast transmitter.

The data link layer hides the above details from the higher layers. To the network layer, it appears as a reliable communication channel which can send and receive data packets as frames.

The Network Layer

The network layer is concerned with the routing of data across the network from one end to another. To do this, the network layer converts the data into packets and ensures that the packets are delivered to their final destination, where they can be converted back into the original data. Network layer protocols are concerned with the following issues:

- The interface between a host and the network.
- The interface between two hosts across the network.
- Routing of packets across the network, including the allocation of a route and handling of congestion
- Correct ordering of packets to reflect the original order of data.
- Collection of statistical information(e.g., number of transmitted packets) for performance measurement and accounting purposes.
- Internetworking: communication between two or more networks.

The network layer hides the above details from the higher layers. To the transport layer, it appears as a uniform data transfer service, regardless of the location of the communicating devices and how they are connected.

The Transport Layer

The aim of the transport layer is to isolate the upper three layers from the network, so that any changes to the network equipment technology will be confined to the lower three layers (i.e., at the node level). Transport layer protocols are concerned with the following issues:

- Establishment and termination of host-to-host connections.
- Efficient and cost-effective delivery of data across the network from one host to another.
- Multiplexing of data, if necessary, to improve use of network bandwidth, and demultiplexing at the other end.
- Splitting of data across multiple network connections, if necessary, to improve throughput, and recombining at the other end.
- Flow control between hosts.
- Addressing of messages to their corresponding connections. The address information appears as a part of the message header.
- Type of service to be provided to the session layer (e.g., error-free versus error-prone connections, whether messages should be delivered in the order received or not).

The transport layer hides the above details from the higher layers. To the session layer, it appears as a customized data transfer service between two hosts, isolating the underlying network technology from it.

The Session Layer

The session layer provides a structured means for data exchange between user processes on communicating hosts. Session layer protocols are concerned with the following issues:

- Negotiating the establishment of a connection(a session) between user processes on communicating hosts, and its subsequent termination. This includes the setting of various communication parameters for the session (e.g., synchronization and control).

- Correct ordering of messages when this function is not performed by the transport layer.
- Recovery from interrupted transport connections, if necessary.
- Grouping of messages into a larger message, if necessary, so that the larger message becomes available at the destination only when its constituent messages have all been delivered successfully.

The session layer hides the above details from the higher layers. To the presentation layer, it appears as an organized communication service between user processes.

The Presentation Layer

The presentation layer provides a mutually-agreeable binary representation of the application data communicated between two user processes. Since there are many ways of encoding application data (e.g., integers, text) into binary data, agreement on a common representation is necessary.

Presentation layer protocols are concerned with issues such as the following:

- Abstract representation of application data.
- Binary representation of application data.
- Conversion between the binary representation of application data and a common format for transmission between peer applications.
- Data compression to better utilize network bandwidth.
- Data encryption as a security measure.

The presentation layer hides the above details from the higher layers. To the application layer, it appears as a universal communication service between user processes, regardless of their system-specific idiosyncrasies, allowing them to converse in a common syntax.

The Application Layer

The application layer is concerned with the semantics of data, i.e., what the data means to applications. The application layer provides standards for supporting a variety of application-independent services. Examples include:

- Virtual terminal standards to allow applications to communicate with different types of terminals in a device-independent manner.
- Message handling system standards used for electronic mail.
- File transfer, access, and management standards for exchanging files or parts thereof between different systems.

Barriers of Communication

There are many barriers to communication and these may occur at any stage in the communication process. Barriers may lead to your message becoming distorted and you therefore risk wasting both time and/or money by causing confusion and misunderstanding. Effective communication involves overcoming these barriers and conveying a clear and concise message.

Common Barriers to Effective Communication

- The use of jargon. Over-complicated, unfamiliar and/or technical terms.
- Emotional barriers and taboos. Some people may find it difficult to express their emotions and some topics may be completely off-limits' or taboo.
- Lack of attention, interest, distractions, or irrelevance to the receiver. (See our page Barriers to Effective Listening for more information).
- Differences in perception and viewpoint.
- Physical disabilities such as hearing problems or speech difficulties.
- Physical barriers to non-verbal communication. Not being able to see the non-verbal cues, gestures, posture and general body language can make communication less effective.

- Language differences and the difficulty in understanding unfamiliar accents.

- Expectations and prejudices which may lead to false assumptions or stereotyping.
  People often hear what they expect to hear rather than what is actually said and jump to incorrect conclusions.

- Cultural differences. The norms of social interaction vary greatly in different cultures, as do the way in which emotions are expressed. For example, the concept of personal space varies between cultures and between different social settings. See our page on Intercultural Awareness for more information.

- A skilled communicator must be aware of these barriers and try to reduce their impact by continually checking understanding and by offering appropriate feedback.

Factors Affecting Communication

Language Barriers

Language and linguistic ability may act as a barrier to communication. However, even when communicating in the same language, the terminology used in a message may act as a barrier if it is not fully understood by the receiver(s). For example, a message that includes a lot of specialist jargon and abbreviations will not be understood by a receiver who is not familiar with the terminology used. Regional colloquialisms and expressions may be misinterpreted or even considered offensive.

Psychological Barriers

Stress management is an important personal skill that affects our interpersonal relationships. Anger is another example of a psychological barrier to communication, when we are angry it is easy to say things that we may later regret and also to misinterpret what others are saying. More generally people with low self-esteem may be less assertive and therefore may not feel comfortable communicating - they may feel shy about saying how they really feel or read negative sub-texts into messages they hear.

Physiological Barriers

A receiver with reduced hearing may not grasp to entirety of a spoken conversation especially if there is significant background noise.

Physical Barriers

Communication is generally easier over shorter distances as more communication channels are available and less technology is required. Although modern technology often serves to reduce the impact of physical barriers, the advantages and disadvantages of each communication channel should be understood so that an appropriate channel can be used to overcome the physical barriers,

Systematic Barriers

Systematic barriers to communication may exist in structures and organisations where there are inefficient or inappropriate information systems and communication channels, or where there is a lack of understanding of the roles and responsibilities for communication.In such organizations, individuals may be unclear of their role in the communication process and therefore not know what is expected of them.

Attitudinal Barriers

Attitudinal barriers to communication may result from personality conflicts, poor management and resistance to change or a lack of motivation. Effective receivers of messages should attempt to overcome their own attitudinal barriers to facilitate effective communication.

The Role and Influence of Mass Media

Mass media is the communication whether written, broadcast, or spoken that reaches a large audience and influence television, radio, advertising, movies, the Internet, newspapers, magazines, and so forth. Mass media is a significant force in modern culture, particularly in America. Sociologists refer to this as a mediated culture where media reflects and creates the culture. Communities and individuals are bombarded constantly with messages from a multitude of sources including TV, billboards, and magazines, to name a few. These messages promote not only products but moods attitudes and a sense of what in and in not important. The current level of media saturation has not always existed television, for example, consisted of primarily three networks, public broadcasting, and a few local independent stations. Today, one can find a television in the poorest of homes, and multiple TVs in most middle-class homes. Not only has availability increased, but programming is increasingly diverse with shows aimed to please all ages, incomes, backgrounds, and attitudes. This widespread availability and exposure makes television the primary focus of most mass-media discussions. More recently, the Internet has increased its role exponentially as more businesses and households.

The limited-effects theory argues that because people generally choose what to watch or read based on what they already believe, media exerts a negligible influence. This theory originated and was tested in the 1940s and 1950s. Studies that examined the ability of media to influence voting found that well-informed people relied more on personal experience, prior knowledge, and their own reasoning.

The class-dominant theory argues that the media reflects and projects the view of minority elite, which controls it. Those people who own and control the corporations that produce media comprise these elite. Networks aim programming at the largest possible audience because the broader the appeal, tire greater the potential purchasing audience and the easier selling air time to advertisers becomes. Thus, news organizations may shy away from negative stories about corporations (especially parent corporations) that finance large advertising campaigns in their newspaper or on their stations

Theorists emphasize that audiences choose to watch among a wide range of options, choose how much to watch, and may choose the mute button or the VCR remote over the programming selected by the network or cable station. Studies of mass media done by sociologist's parallel text-reading and interpretation research completed by linguists (people who study language). Both groups of researchers find that when people approach material, whether written text or media images and messages, they interpret that material based on their own knowledge and experience. Thus, when researchers ask different groups to explain the meaning of a particular song or video, the groups produce widely divergent interpretations based on age, gender, race, ethnicity, and religious background. Therefore, culturalist theorists claim that, while a few elite in large corporations may exert significant control over what information media produces and distributes, personal perspective plays a more powerful role in how the audience members interpret those messages.

Concept, Function and Importance

The importance of knowledge as a basis for social power has been noted by a number of scholars but less well appreciated is the fact that control of knowledge is central to development and maintenance of power. In present-day society, large scale organizations in both public and private sectors are structured to carefully control both the assimilation and dissemination of information. The rapidly growing data-processing agencies represent overt recognition of the role of information and its control in modern social organization. It is still important to study the micro-processes of mass communication, but given the growing importance of information control in society, it appears equally important to take a macro-view of mass media as interdependent parts of a total social system in which they share facets of controlling, and being controlled by, other subsystems.

The examination of the nature of the process by which this transmission occurs and the systemic relations among the various subsystems, is a major focal point. One should not assume from the above that social control is the only function served by mass communication, but rather that all communication processes have a control function within them, either latent or manifest. Along with deepening involvement of science in public decision-making has come an increased amount of science content in mass media. Most of this content may be described as "knowledge of rather than "knowledge about." "Knowledge of refers to familiarity with a topic or events surrounding it, whereas "knowledge about" includes analytic and formal knowledge. One reason for this concentration on "knowledge of in science, as well as in most specialized knowledge areas, stems from the limitations of the media system and the controls exerted on media personnel.

Media and science systems do not accommodate each other as readily as, say, media and political systems. Norms for entry and participation in political and science groups are quite different. Accumulation of knowledge is fundamental to growth and development of a scientific field, and control of knowledge flow is crucial to the field's legitimacy and survival. A scientific group feels it has arrived when it possesses a unique body of knowledge which is considered necessary and can be dispensed to the nonscientific world, that is, other subsystems, in a therapeutic fashion.

Mass Media and Education

Communication is important, because every administrative function and activity involves some form of direct or indirect communication. Whether planning and organizing or leading and monitoring, school administrators communicate with and through other people. This implies that every person's communication skills affect both personal and organizational effectiveness one of the most inhibiting forces to organizational effectiveness is a lack of effective communication. Moreover good communication skills are very important to ones success as a school administrator. Communication can be defined as the process of transmitting information and understanding from one person to another. The word communication is derived from the Latin word, communications, which means common. The definition underscores the fact that unless a common understanding results from the exchange of information, there is no communication. Two common elements in every communication exchange are the sender and the receiver.

The sender initiates the communication. In a school, the sender is a person who has a need or desire to convey an idea or concept to others. The receiver is the individual to whom the message is sent. The sender encodes the idea by selecting words, symbols, or gestures with which to compose a message. The message is the outcome of the encoding, which takes the form of verbal, nonverbal, or written language. The message is sent through a medium or channel, which is the carrier of the communication. The medium can be a face-to-face conversation, telephone call, e-mail, or written report. The receiver decodes the received message into meaningful information. Finally, feedback occurs when the receiver responds to the sender's message and returns the message to the sender. Feedback allows the sender to determine whether the message has been received and understood.

The elements in the communication process determine the quality of communication. A problem in any one of these elements can reduce communication effectiveness (Keyton,2011). For example, information must be encoded into a message that can be understood as the sender intended. Selection of the particular medium for transmitting the message can be critical, because there are many choices. For written media, administrator or other organization member may choose from memos, letters, reports, bulletin boards, handbooks, newsletters, and the like. For verbal media, choices include face-to-face conversations, telephone, computer, public address systems, closed-circuit television, tape-recorded messages, sound/slide shows, e-mail, and so on. Nonverbal gestures, facial expressions, body position, and even clothing can transmit messages.

Barriers and Solution

Process Barriers

Every step in the communication process is necessary for effective and good communication. Blocked steps become barriers.

- Sender barrier
- Encoding barrier
- Medium barrier
- Decoding barrier

- Receiver barrier
- Feedback barrier

Physical Barriers

Any number of physical distractions can interfere with the effectiveness of communication, including a telephone call, drop-in visitors, distances between people, walls, and static on the radio. People often take physical barriers for granted, but sometimes they can be removed. For example, an inconveniently positioned wall can be removed. Interruptions such as telephone calls and drop-in visitors can be removed by issuing instructions to a secretary. An appropriate choice of media can overcome distance barriers between people.

Semantic Barriers

The words we choose, how we use them, and the meaning we attach to them cause many communication barriers. The problem is semantic, or the meaning of the words we use. The same word may mean different things to different people. Words and phrases such as efficiency, increased productivity, management prerogatives, and just cause may mean one thing to a school administrator, and something entirely different to a staff member. Technology also plays a part in semantic barriers to communication. Today's complex school systems are highly specialized.

Psychosocial Barriers

Three important concepts are associated with psychological and social barriers fields of experience, filtering and psychological distance. Fields of experience include people's backgrounds, perceptions, values, biases, needs, and expectations. Senders can encode and receivers decode messages only in the context of their fields of experience. When the sender's field of experience overlaps very little with the receiver's, communication becomes difficult. Filtering means that more often than not we see and hear what we are emotionally tuned in to see and hear. Filtering is caused by our own needs and interests, which guide our listening. Psychosocial barriers often involve a psychological distance between people that is similar to actual physical distanced.

- Sincerity
- Empathy
- Self-perception
- Role perception
- Efforts to distort the message
- Images
- Vehicle for message
- Ability to communicate
- Listening ability
- Culture
- Tradition
- Conditioning
- Noise and feed back

CHAPTER 3

NEW HORIZONS IN ICT

The most important educational resource is people-teachers. However, it has to be recognized that in the present and the foreseeable future, economic and political restrictions are unlikely to be such that adequate supplies of suitably trained teachers will be available to completely fill the need for them. When human resources are inadequate, it is often easier to procure and provide technological solutions and it is most fortunate that in special education, technology can play a highly beneficial role. Although economic restrictions can affect access to technology, it can represent a good investment.

Recent Trends in the Area of ICT

10 Global Trends in ICT and Education

- **Mobile Learning**: New advances in hardware and software are making mobile "smart phones" indispensible tools. Just as cell phones have leapfrogged fixed line technology in the telecommunications industry, it is likely that mobile devices with internet access and computing capabilities will soon overtake personal computers as the information appliance of choice in the classroom.

- **Cloud Computing**: Applications are increasingly moving off of the stand alone desk top computer and increasingly onto server farms accessible through the Internet. The implications of this trend for education systems are huge; they will make cheaper information appliances available which do not require the processing power or size of the PC. The challenge will be providing the ubiquitous connectivity to access information sitting in the "cloud".

- **One-to-One Computing**: The trend in classrooms around the world is to provide an information appliance to every learner and create learning environments that assume universal access to the technology. Whether the hardware invoked is one laptop per child (OLPC), or increasingly-a net computer, smart phone, or the re-emergence of the tablet, classrooms should prepare for the universal availability of personal learning devices

- **Ubiquitous   Learning**: With the emergence of increasingly robust connectivity infrastructure and cheaper computers, school systems around the world are developing the ability to provide learning opportunities to students "anytime, anywhere". This trend requires a rethinking of the traditional 40 minute lesson. In Addition to hardware and Internet access, it requires the availability of virtual mentors or teachers, and/or opportunities for peer to peer and self-paced, deeper learning.

- **Gaming**: A recent survey by the Pew Internet and American Life Project per the Horizon Report found that massively multiplayer and other online game experience is extremely common among young people and that games offer an opportunity for increased social interaction and civic engagement among youth. The phenomenal success of games with a focus on active participation, built in incentives and interaction suggests that current educational methods are not falling short and that educational games could more effectively attract the interest and attention of learners.

- **Personalized   Learning**: Education systems are increasingly investigating the use of technology to better understand a student's knowledge base from prior learning and to tailor teaching to both address learning gaps as well as learning styles.This focus transforms a classroom from one that teaches to the middle to one that adjusts content and pedagogy based on individual student needs - both strong and weak.

- **Redefinition of Learning Spaces**: The ordered classroom of 30 desks in rows of 5 may quickly become a relic of the industrial age as schools around the world are rethinking the most appropriate learning environments to foster collaborative, cross-disciplinary, students centered learning. Concepts such as greater use of light, colors, circular tables, individual spaces for students and teachers, and smaller open learning spaces for project-based learning are increasingly emphasized.

- **Teacher-generated Open Content**: OECD school systems are increasingly empowering teachers and networks of teachers to both identify and create the learning resources that they find most effective in the classroom. Many online texts allow teachers to edit, add to, or otherwise customize material for their own purposes, so that their students receive a tailored copy that exactly suits the style and pace of the course. These resources in many cases complement the official textbook and may, in the years to come, supplant the textbook as the primary learning source for students. Such activities often challenge traditional notions of intellectual property and copyright.

- **Smart Portfolio Assessment**: The collection, management, sorting, and retrieving of data related to learning will help teachers to better understand learning gaps and customize content and pedagogical approaches. Also, assessment is increasingly moving toward frequent formative assessments which lend itself to real-time data and less on high-pressure exams as the mark of excellence. Tools are increasingly available to students to gather their work together in a kind of online portfolio; whenever they add a tweet, blog post, or photo to any online service, it will appear in their personal portfolio which can be both peer and teacher assessed.

- **Teacher Managers/Mentors**: The role of the teacher in the classroom is being transformed from that of the font of knowledge to an instructional manager helping to guide students through individualized learning pathways, identifying relevant learning resources, creating collaborative learning opportunities, and providing insight and support both during formal class time and outside of the designated 40 minute instruction period. This shift is easier said than done and ultimately the success or failure of technology projects in the classroom hinge on the human factor and the willingness of a teacher to step into unchartered territory. These trends are expected to continue and to challenge many of the delivery models fundamental to formal education as it is practiced in most countries.

Interactive Video

Interactive video is a "two-way video conference network system". Interactive videos present new ways of using the television, including on-demand video, two-way conference and phone-in programs. Interactive television users are able to select subtitles or captions, choose from different audio and video streams, communicate by email or telephone during a broadcast and access supplementary materials on screen while viewing the video instructors using interactive television as a teaching tool make use of a variety of multimedia tools, such as cameras and microphones, to promote interaction with participants. Unique elements linked to a live television broadcast, such as live-to-air questions, answer sessions with the presenter, faxing assignments and telephone conversations; define interactive television and videos in an educational setting.

The ability to display a combination of video and computer images and features makes interactive videos a unique educational tool Teachers living in remote or rural communities have the opportunity to engage in professional development sessions without traveling, These professional development sessions are favored by teachers due to the reduced amount of time away from home and classroom and the money saved by not traveling long distances. Interactive videos can present options for students who live in secluded regions and fell isolated from available resources. Interactive television can allow students to tune into learning opportunities via a broadcast system.Learning in context is also a possibility thanks to interactive television.

Interactive television is often used as a medium for distance education. Hilgenber and Tolone(2000) found that students were generally satisfied with their course and the dialogue with the instructor, which was made possible with interactive elements. The features of interactive television, such as phone in conversations or live-to air question periods, have proven to be a motivational factor for students because they are more motivated to engage in the discussion during an interactive session and to prepare a quality response interactive video gaming was an effective tool for enhancing student motivation and mood for effective physical exercise are interested. Physical educators will find that interactive gaming is an effective way to motivate those students who are interested in video games and are less physically active and is an effective way to engage young, game –literate students on pedestrian safety. Without having to leave the safety and confines of the classroom, students could engage in videos containing real life footage students were more able to transfer knowledge than had they been engaged in a simulated activity

Interactive television provides students with just-in-time support a feature that cannot be made possible with pre-recorded educational videos. Students of interactive television also score higher than students of taped video because they have the advantage of face–to-face interaction with the instructor and received immediate feedback. While interactive television presents itself as a beneficial tool for learning, it is often not used the way in it is intended to be used. Education facilities invest a lot of money into installing interactive television equipment but extra efforts are needed to ensure teachers know how to use it through professional development and teachers also need to feel positive about it as a learning tool.

Research is supportive of student–centered learning for distance education because of its ability to engage learners and increase student's success, but interactive television instruction are still inclined to instruct from a teacher–centered approach. The use of interactive television for distance impede student learning and interaction with the instructor students felt that instructors of interactive television were not taking an active role in delivering content and were disengaged.

Interactive White Board

Interactive whiteboard (IWB) is a large interactive display that connects to a computer. A projector projects the computer's desktop onto the board's surface where users control the computer using a pen, finger, stylus, or other device. The board is typically mounted to a wall or floor stand. They are used in a variety of settings, including classrooms at all levels of education, in corporate board rooms and work groups, in training rooms for professional sports coaching, in broadcasting studios, and others. The first interactive whiteboards were designed and manufactured for use in the office. They were developed by Xerox Pare around 1990. This board was used in small group meetings and round-tables.

The interactive whiteboard industry was expected to reach sales of US$1 billion worldwide by 2008; one of every seven classrooms in the world was expected to feature an interactive whiteboard by 2011 according to market research by Future source Consulting

Uses for Interactive Whiteboards may Includes

- Running software that is loaded onto the connected PC, such as a web browsers or other software used in the classroom.
- Capturing and saving notes written on a whiteboard to the connected PC
- Capturing notes written on a graphics tablet connected to the whiteboard
- Controlling the PC from the white board using click and drag, markup which annotates a program or presentation
- Using OCR software to translate cursive writing on a graphics tablet into text
- Using an Audience Response System so that presenters can poll a classroom audience or conduct quizzes, capturing feedback onto the whiteboard

An interactive whiteboard (IWB) device is connected to a computer via USB or a serial port cable, or else wirelessly via Bluetooth or wireless. A device driver is usually installed on the attached computer so that the interactive whiteboard can act as a Human Input Device (HID), like a mouse. The computer's video output is connected to a digital projector so that images may be projected on the interactive whiteboard surface.

The user then calibrates the whiteboard image by matching the position of the projected image in reference to the whiteboard using a pointer as necessary. After this, the pointer or other crevices may be used to activate programs, buttons and menus from the whiteboard itself, just as one would ordinarily do with a mouse. If text input is required, user can invoke an on-screen keyboard or, if the whiteboard software provides for this, utilize handwriting recognition. This makes it unnecessary to go to the computer keyboard to enter text.

Common Types of Operation

- Operation of a resistive touch-based interactive whiteboard
- Operation of a infrared scan (IR touch) whiteboard
- Operation of an electromagnetic pen-based interactive whiteboard
- Operation of a portable ultrasonic, IR pen-based interactive white borax.
- Operation of a Wiimote/IR-based interactive whiteboard
- Operation of a virtual whiteboard via an interactive projector

Classroom Uses

In some classrooms, interactive whiteboards have replaced traditional whiteboards or flipcharts, or video/media systems such as a DVD player and TV combination. Even where traditional boards are used, the IWB often supplements them by connecting to a school network digital video distribution system. In other cases, IWBs interact with online shared annotation and drawing environments such as interactive vector based graphical websites.

Brief instructional blocks can be recorded for review by students will see the exact presentation that occurred in the classroom with the teacher's audio input. This can help transform learning and instruction. One recent use of the IWB is in shared reading lessons. Mimic books, for instance, allow teachers to project children's books onto the interactive whiteboard with book-like interactivity.

Dixons city Academy in the North of England was the first noncollege or university learning environment to make use of interactive whiteboard. By combining classroom response with an interactive whiteboard system, teachers can present material and receive feedback from students in order to direct instruction more effectively or else to carry out formal assessments. For example, a student may both solve a puzzle involving math concepts on the interactive whiteboard and later demonstrate his or her knowledge on a test delivered via the classroom response system. Some classroom response software can organize and develop activities and tests aligned with State standards.

Video Conferencing

Video Conferencing (VC) is the conduct of a videoconference (also known as a video conference or video teleconference) by a set of telecommunication technologies which two or more locations to communicative by simultaneous two-way video and audio transmissions. It has also been called 'visual collaboration' and its type of groupware. Videoconferencing differs from videophone calls in that it's designed to serve a conference or multiple locations rather than individuals. It is an intermediate form of video telephony, first used commercially in Germany during the late-1930s and later in the United States during the early 1970s.

With the introduction of relatively low cost, high capacity broadband telecommunication services in the late 1990s, coupled with powerful computing processors and video compression   techniques, videoconferencing has   made   significant   inroads in business, education, medicine and media. Video conferencing uses audio and video telecommunications to bring people at different sites together. Besides the audio and visual transmission of meeting activities, allied video conferencing technologies can be used to share documents and display information on whiteboards.

Simple analogue videophone communication could be established as early as the invention of the television. Such an antecedent usually consisted of two closed-circuit television systems connected via coax cable or radio.

The components required for a video conferencing system include:

- **Video Input**: Video Camera or Webcam
- **Video Output:** Computer Monitor, Television or Projector

Audio Input: Microphones, CD/DVD player, cassette player, or any other source of Pre-Amp audio outlet.

Data Transfer: Analog or digital telephone network, LAN or internet

Computer: A data processing unit that ties together the other components, does the compressing and decompressing, and initiates and maintains the data linkage via the network.

Two kinds of video conferencing systems

- Dedicated Systems
- Desktop Systems
- WebRTC Platforms

Impact on Education

Video conferencing provides students with the opportunity to learn by participating in two-way communication forums. Furthermore, teachers and lectures worldwide can be brought to remote or otherwise isolated educational facilities. Students from diverse communities and backgrounds can come together to learn about one another, although language barriers will continue to persist. Such students are able to explore, communicate, analyse and share information and ideas with one another. Through video conferencing, students can visit other parts of the world to speak with their peers, and visit museums and educational facilities. Such virtual field trips can provide enriched learning opportunities to students, especially those in geographically isolated locations, and to the economically disadvantaged. Small schools can use these technologies to pool resources and provide courses, such an in foreign languages, which could not otherwise be offered.

A few examples of benefits that video conferencing can provide in campus environments includes

- Faculty members keeping in touch with classes while attending conferences
- Guest lecturers brought in classes from other institutions
- Researchers collaborating with colleagues at other institutions on a regular basis without loss of time due to travel
- Schools with multiple composes, collaborating and sharing professors
- Schools from two separate nations engaging in cross-cultural exchanges
- Faculty members participating in thesis defences at other institutions
- Administrators on tight schedules collaborating on budget preparation from different parts of campus
- Faculty committee auditioning scholarship candidates
- Researchers answering questions about grant proposals from agencies or review committees
- Student interviews with an employers in other cities and Teleseminars

M-Learning

M-learning or mobile learning is defined as "learning across multiple contexts, through social and content interactions, using personal electronic devices. A form of distance education, m-learners use mobile device educational technology at their time convenience. M-learning technologies include handheld computers, MP3 players, notebooks, mobile phones and tablets. M-learning focuses on the mobility of the learner, interacting with portable technologies. Using mobile tools for creating learning aids and materials becomes an important part of informal learning.

M-learning is convenient in that it is accessible from virtually anywhere. Sharing is almost instantaneous among everyone using the same content, which leads to the reception of instant feedback and tips. This highly active process has proven to increase exam scores from the fiftieth to the seventieth percentile, and cut the dropout rate in technical fields. M-learning also brings strong portability by replacing books and notes with small devices, filled with tailored learning contents.

Mobile learning is the delivery of learning, education or learning support on mobile phones, PDAs or tablets. E-Learning has provided the ability for traditional learning to break out of the classroom setting and for students to learn at home. New mobile technology, such as hand-held based devices, is playing a large role in redefining how we receive information. The Recent advances in mobile technology are changing the primary purpose of mobile devices from making or receiving calls to retrieving the latest information on any subject.

Classroom applications combine the use of handheld computers, PDAs, smart phones or handheld voting systems(such as clickers) with traditional resources. Mobile devices in the classroom can be used to enhance group collaboration among students through communication applications, interactive displays, and video features.

- Existing mobile technology can replace cumber some resources such as textbooks, visual aids, and presentation technology.
- Interactive and multi-mode technology allows students to engage and manipulate information.

- Mobile Device features with W1FI capabilities allow for on-demand access to information.
- Access to classroom activities and information on mobile devices provides a continuum for learning inside and outside the classroom.

M-learning in the context of work can embrace a variety of different forms of learning. It has been defined as the "processes of coming to know, and of being able to operate successfully in, and across, new and ever changing contexts, including learning for, at and through work, by means of mobile device.

- M -learning for work
- M-learning at and through work
- Cross-contextual m-learning

Lifelong Learning and Self-learning

Mobile technologies and approaches, i.e. mobile-assisted language learning (MALL), are also used to assist in language learning. For instance handheld computers, cell phones, and podcasting **(Hark off Kayes, 2008)** have been used to help people acquire and develop language skills.

It is important to bring new technology into the classroom.

- Devices used are more lightweight than books and PCs.
- Mobile learning can be used to diversify the types of learning activities students partake in (or a blended learning approach).
- Mobile learning supports the learning process rather than being integral to it. Mobile learning can be a useful add-on tool for students with special needs. However, for SMS and MMS this might be dependent on the students' specific disabilities or difficulties involved.
- Mobile learning can be used as a 'hook' to re-engage disaffected youth.

Benefits

- Relatively inexpensive opportunities, as the cost of mobile devices are significantly less than PCs and laptops
- Multimedia content delivery and creation options
- Continuous and situated learning support
- Decrease in training costs
- Potentially a more rewarding learning experience
- New opportunities for traditional educational institutions
- Readily available a/synchronous learning experience

Challenges

Technical Challenges

- Connectivity and battery life
- Screen size and key size
- Meeting required bandwidth for nonstop/fast streaming
- Number of file/asset formats supported by a specific device
- Content security or copyright issue from authoring group .
- Multiple standards, multiple screen sizes, multiple operating systems
- Reworking existing E-Learning materials for mobile platforms
- Limited memory'

Social Media

Social media are computer-mediated tools that allow people or companies to create, share, or exchange information, career interests, ideas, and pictures/videos in virtual communities and networks. Social media is defined as "a group of Internet-based applications that build on the ideological and technological foundations of Web 2.0 and that allow the creation and exchange of user-generated content. Furthermore, social media depend on mobile and web- based technologies to create highly interactive platforms through which individuals and communities share, co-create, discuss, and modify user-generated content. They introduce substantial and pervasive changes to communication between businesses, organizations, communities, Diagram depicting the many different types of social media and individuals. These changes are the focus of the emerging field of techno self studies. Social media differ from traditional or industrial media in many ways, including quality," reach, frequency, usability, immediacy, and permanence. Social media has been broadly defined to refer to 'the many relatively inexpensive and widely accessible electronic tools that enable anyone to publish and access information, collaborate on a common effort, or build relationships.

Classification of Social Media

Social media technologies take on many different forms including blogs, business networks, enterprise social networks, forums, micro blogs, photo sharing, products/services review, social bookmarking, social gaming, social networks, video sharing, and virtual worlds. Some social media sites have greater virality-defined as a greater likelihood that users will reshape content posted (by another user) to their social network. Many social media sites provide specific functionality to help users reshare content-for example, Twitter's retweet button, Pinterest pin or Tumblr's reblog function. Businesses may have a particular interest in viral marketing; nonprofit organisations and activists may have similar interests in virality.

Framework of Social Media

- Identity
- Conversations
- Sharing

- Presence
- Relationships
- Reputation
- Groups

Community Radio

Community radio is a radio service offering a third model of radio broadcasting in addition to commercial and public broadcasting. Community stations serve geographic communities and communities of interest. They broadcast content that is popular and relevant to a local, specific audience but is often overlooked by commercial or mass-media broadcasters. Community radio stations are operated, owned, and influenced by the communities they serve. They are generally nonprofit and provide a mechanism for enabling individuals, groups, and communities to tell their own stories, to share experiences and, in a media-rich world, to become creators and contributors of media.

In many parts of the world, community radio acts as a vehicle for the community and voluntary sector, civil society, agencies, NGOs and citizens to work in partnership to further community development aims, in addition to broadcasting. There is legally defined community radio (as a distinct broadcasting sector) in many countries, such as France, Argentina, South Africa, Australia and Ireland. Much of the legislation has included phrases such as "social benefit", "social objectives" and "social gain" as part of the definition.

Vision, Philosophy and Status

Modern community radio stations serve their listeners by offering a variety of content that is not necessarily provided by the larger commercial radio stations. Community radio outlets may carry news and information programming geared toward the local area.

Model

Two philosophical approaches to community radio exist, although the models are not mutually exclusive. One emphasizes service and community-mindedness, focusing on what the station can do for the community. The other stresses involvement and participation by the listener. In the service model locality is valued; community radio, as a third tier, can provide content focused on a more local or particular community than a larger operation. Sometimes, though, providing syndicated content not already available within the station's service area is viewed as public service.

Gyan Dharshan

DD Gyandarshan is an educational television channel that relays programmes from various Doordarshan Kendras in different Languages. The Educational television channel is organized and administered by NCERT, IGNOU and the National Institute of Open Schools. Educational TV is one of the priority areas for Doordarshan. Curriculum based programmes are produced with active involvement of state educational administrators and teachers and are telecast from Delhi, Mumbai and Chennai. Satellite based enrichment programmes for school children are produced by the State Institutes of Educational Technology (SIET).

DD Gyandarshan India is an exclusive Educational TV channel of India. IGNOU, Ministry of Human Resources Development and Prasar Bharti started the channel in January 2000. This channel provides a blejnd of core curriculum based programs in the areas of primary, secondary, higher, distance, technical and vocational education.

Education Media Research Centres (EMRC) and Audio Visual Research Centres at different places produce programmes for university students. These enrichment programmes provide education within the reach of students in small towns and villages. The programmes are telecast on Gyandarshan from 6 am to midnight and also on DD-1 and DD-2.

Gyandarshan-I beams round the clock programmes acquired from UGC, National Council for Educational Research and Training, Central Institute for Educational Technology, State Institute of Research and Training and IGNOU. Aka Eklavya-Gyandarshan-lll channel dedicated to technical education was started on January 26,2003, in collaboration with the Department of Technical Education of the HRD Ministry and NTs with IT, Delhi as the nodal point. The channel airing programmes originating from different IITs for the benefit of students pursuing studies in Technology and Engineering has marked the beginning of a new era in the spread of Technical Education in the country. One of the most popular programmes of the channel is Nitttr, which is an educational program that keeps pace with the improvement in the areas of technology, hosted by National Institute of Technical Teachers Training and Research.

Gyan Vani

Gyan Vani is an educational FM radio station in several cities of India. Gyan Vani stations operate as a "media cooperative with the day-to-day programmes being contributed by various educational institutions, NGOs, government and semi-government organizations, UN agencies, ministries such as Agriculture, Environment, Health, Women and Child Welfare, Science & Technology, etc. besides national level institutions such as NCERT, NIOS and state open universities. Each Gyan Vani station has a range of about 60 km and covers an entire city including the adjoining rural areas. The medium of broadcast is English, Hindi or language of the region.Gyan Vani FM radio uses stereophonic FM transmitters, and professionals operate the radio stations. Each nodal centre is provided with media from Indira Gandhi National Open University's (IGNOU) Electronic Media Production Centre. The centre serves purposes of production, dissemination and transmission of educational material. The facilities available at the media production centre are shared with various educational and training institutions, state open universities, central and state government ministries or departments, nongovernmental organizations, corporate bodies and other sectors.

The idea was to use the audio video studios available with the educational institutions for producing the programme, and use the AIR or the Doordarsan, public broadcasters' towers and technical facilities for transmission. A memorandum of understanding was signed between IGNOU and Prasar Bharati to share the towers. But as of 2013 there are 37 stations functioning. But the original concepts of localized broadcasts have been given a go by and most of them are relaying the Delhi programmes. The second phase of radio privatisation even though reserved one frequency for education, neither the MHRD, the nodal ministry nor IGNOU, has taken any interest in pursuing the network.

Blog

A blog is a discussion or informational site published on the world Wide Web consisting of discrete typically displayed in reverse chronological order.

MOOC

A massive open online course (MOOC) is an online course aimed at unlimited participation and open access via the web. In addition to traditional course materials such as filmed lectures, readings, and problem sets, many MOOCs provide interactive user forums to support community interactions among students, professors, and teaching assistants, MOOCs are a recent and widely researched development in distance educations/which were first introduced in 2008 and emerged as a popular mode of learning in 2012. Early MOOCs often emphasized open-access features, such as open licensing of content, structure and learning goals, to promote the reuse and remixing of resources. Some later MOOCs use closed licenses for their course materials while maintaining free access for students.

Early Approaches

The first MOOCs emerged from the open educational resources (OER) movement. The term MOOC was coined in 2008 by Dave Cormier of the University of Prince Edward Island in response to a course called Connectives and Connective Knowledge (also known as CCK08).

Emergence of Innovative Courses

Early MOOCs such as CCK08 and dsl06 used innovative pedagogy, with distributed learning materials rather than a video-lecture format, and a focus on education and learning, and digital story telling respectively. A range of courses have emerged. There was a real question of whether this would work for humanities and social science. However, psychology and philosophy courses are among Courser's most popular. Student feedback and completion rates suggest that they are as successful as math and science courses even though the corresponding completion rates are lower.

Course developers could charge licensing fees for educational institutions that use its materials. Introductory or gateway courses and some remedial courses may earn the most fees. Free introductory courses may attract new students to follow-on fee-charging classes. Blended courses supplement MOOC material with face-to-face instruction. Providers can charge employers for recruiting its students. Students may be able to pay to take a proctored exam to earn transfer credit at a degree-granting university, or for certificates of completion.

Challenges and Criticisms

The MOOC Guide suggests five possible challenges for MOOC

1. Relying on user-generated content can create a chaotic learning environment
2. Digital literacy is necessary to make use of the online materials.
3. The time and effort required from participants may exceed what students are willing to commit to a free online course.
4. Once the course is released, content will be reshaped and reinterpreted by the massive body, making the course trajectory difficult for instructors to control.
5. Participants must self-regulate and set their own goals

These general challenges in effective MOOC development are accompanied by criticism by journalists and academics.

Whatsapp

WhatsApp TV messenger is a proprietary cross-platform instant messaging client for smartphones. It uses the Internet to send text messages, documents, images, video, user location and audio media messages to other users using standard cellular mobile numbers. As of February 2016 Whatsapp had a user base of one billion making it the second-most popular messaging application.

WhatsApp Inc., was founded in 2009 by Brian Acton and Jan Koum, both former employees of Yahoo After Koum and Acton left yahoo in September 2007, the duo traveled to south america as break from work. At point they applied for jobs at facebook but were rejected.

In June 2009, Apple launched push notifications, letting developers ping users when they were not using an app. **Koum** updated WhatsApp so that each time the user changed their statuses, it would ping everyone in the user's network. WhatsApp was switched from a free to paid service to avoid growing too fast, mainly because the primary cost was sending verification texts to users

Twitter

Twitter is an online social networking service that enables users to send and read short 140 character messages called "tweets". Registered users can read and post tweets, but those who are unregistered can only read them. Users access Twitter through the website interface, SMS or mobile device app. Twitter Inc. is based in San Francisco and has more than 25 offices around the world.

Twitter was created in March 2006 by Jack Dorsey, Evan Williams, Biz Stone, and Noah Glass and launched in July 2006. The service rapidly gained worldwide popularity, with more than 100 million users posting 340 million tweets a day in 2012. Twitter was one of the ten most visited websites and has been described as "the SMS of the Internet".

The original project code name for the service was twttr, an idea that Williams later ascribed to Noah Glass, inspired by Flickr and the five character length of American SMS short codes. The decision was also partly due to the fact that domain twitter.com was already in use, and it was six months after the launch of twttr that the crew purchased the domain and changed the name of the service to Twitter.

Twitter announced its own integrated photo sharing service that enables users to upload a photo and attach it to a Tweet right from Twitter.com. Users now also have the ability to add pictures to Twitter's search by adding hash tags to the tweet. Twitter also plans to provide photo galleries designed to gather and syndicate all photos that a user has uploaded on Twitter and third party services such as TwitPic.

A Twitterbot is a computer program that automatically posts on Twitter, they are programmed to tweet, retweet and follow other accounts. According to a recent report, there were 20 million, fewer than 5%, of accounts on Twitter that were fraudulent in 2013. These fake accounts are often used to build large follower populations quickly for advertisers, while others respond to tweets that include a certain word or phrase. Twitter's wide open application programming interface and cloud servers make it possible for twitter bots existence within the social networking site.

Twitter has been adopted as a communication and learning tool in educational settings mostly in colleges and universities. It has been used as a backchannel to promote student interactions, especially in large lecture courses. Research has found that using Twitter in college courses helps students communicate with each other and faculty, promotes informal learning, allows shy students a forum for increased participation, increases student engagement, and improves overall course grades.

Positive and Negative Effects of Twitter

1. People around the world are taking advantage of social media as one of their key components of communication.

2. With the expansion of social media networks there are many positive and negative alternatives. As the use of Twitter increases, its influence impacts users as well. The potential role of Twitter as a means of both service feedback and a space in which mental health can be openly discussed and considered from a variety of perspectives.

3. On the other hand, there can be negatives that arise from the use of social media.

4. Although social media can be beneficial, it is important to understand the negative consequences as well.

Virtual Classroom

In object-oriented programming a virtual class is a nested inner class whose functions and member variables can be overridden and redefined by subclasses of the outer class. Virtual classes are analogous to virtual functions. The run time type of a virtual class depends on the run time type of an object of the outer class. A run time instance type of the outer class object not only decides on the polymorphic type of its own type object, but also on a whole family tree of virtual class members.

Purpose

Virtual classes solve the extensibility problem of extending data abstraction with new functions and representations. Like virtual functions, virtual classes follow the same rules of definition, overriding, and reference. When derived class inherits from a base class, it must define or override the virtual inner classes it inherited from the base class. An object of the child class may be referred to by a reference or pointer of the parent class type or the child class type. A method with an object argument has access to the object's virtual classes. The method can use the virtual classes of its arguments to create instances and declare variables. Virtual classes of different instances are not compatible.

Virtual Learning Environment

A Virtual Learning Environment (VLE) is a web-based platform for the digital aspects of courses of study, usually within educational institutions. VLEs typically: allow participants to be organized into cohorts, groups and roles; present resources, activities and interactions within a course structure; provide for the different stages of assessment; report on participation; and have some level of integration with other institutional systems. The following are the basic or the main components required for a virtual learning environment or online education curriculum to take place.

A VLE may include some or all of the following elements:

- The course syllabus
- Administrative information about the course: prerequisites, credits, registration, payments, physical sessions, and contact information for the instructor.
- A notice board for current information about the ongoing course

- The basic content of some or all of the course; the complete course for distance learning applications, or some part of it, when used as a portion of a conventional course. This normally includes material such as copies of lecture in the form of text, audio, or video presentations, and the supporting visual presentations

- Additional resources, either integrated or as links to outside resources. This typically consists of supplementary reading, or innovative equivalents for it.

- Self-assessment quizzes or analogous devices, normally scored automatically

- Formal assessment functions, such as examinations, essay submission, or presentation of projects. This now frequently includes components to support peer assessment

- Support for communications, including e-mail, threaded discussions, chat rooms, Twitter and other media, sometimes with the instructor or an assistant acting as moderator. Additional elements include wikis, blogs, RSS and 3D virtual learning spaces.

- Links to outside sources – pathways to all other online learning spaces are linked via the VLE (Virtual Learning Environment).

- Management of access rights for instructors, their assistants, course support staff, and Students

- Documentation and statistics as required for institutional administration and quality control

- Authoring tools for creating the necessary documents by the instructor, and, usually, submissions by the students

- Provision for the necessary hyperlinks to create a unified presentation to the students.

The virtual learning environment supports an exchange of information between a user and the learning institute he or she is currently enrolled in through digital mediums like e-mail, chat rooms, web 2.0 sites or a forum thereby helping convey information to any part of the world with just a single click.

The terms virtual learning environment (VLE) and learning platform are generically used to describe a range of integrated web based applications that provide teachers, learners, parents and others involved in education with information, tools and resources to support and enhance educational delivery and management.

Student Accessibility Features

A virtual learning environment offers a learning system with many components, with added advantage of computer based learning and teaching space. One of the process to enhance the learning experience was the virtual resource room, which is student centered, works in a self-paced format, and which encourages students to take responsibility for their own learning. In virtual mode, the materials are available in the form of computer aided learning program, lecture notes, special self-assessment module. Another mechanism for student to student interactions in a form of simple discussion forum is by using a novel link Cyber tutor. This allows the students with an email account to connect with course content and the staff with their doubts and related questions. The students are able to contact the staff without a face to face visit which saves the on campus time.

Students can discuss about the exams, lab reports, posters, lectures, and technical help with downloading materials. The evaluation of the use of Virtual resource room is done by surveys, focus groups and online feedback forms. The students have 24 hours of access to the learning material in a day which suits their varied life styles.

Blended Learning

Blended learning is a formal education program in which a student learns at least in part through delivery of content and instruction via digital and online media with some element of student control over time, place, path, or pace. While students still attend "brick-and-mortar" schools, face-to-face classroom methods are combined with computer-mediated activities. Blended learning is also used in professional development and training settings, as it can be used to translate knowledge into a particular skill that is useful and practical for a specific job.

The terms blended learning or hybrid learning, technology-mediated instruction, web- enhanced instruction and mixed-mode instruction are often used interchangeably. The concept of blended learning has been around for a long time, but its terminology was not firmly established until about the start of 21st century. Currently, use of the term blended learning mostly involves, "combining Internet and digital media with established classroom forms that require the physical co-presence of teacher and students."

Technology based training emerged as an alternative to instructor-led training in the 1960s on mainframes and minicomputers. The major advantage that blended learning offers is scale, whereas one instructor can only teach so many people. The major challenge was the expense required to make this work. The Modern blended learning is delivered online, although CDROMs could feasibly still be used if a learning management system meets an institution's standards. Some examples of channels through which online blending learning can be delivered include webcasting and online video.

Blended learning can generally be classified into six models

- **Face-to-face Driver** where the teacher drives the instruction and augments with digital tools.
- **Rotation** students cycle through a schedule of independent online study and face-to-face classroom time.
- **Flex** Most of the curriculum is delivered via a digital platform and teachers are available for Face-to-face consultation and support.
- **Labs** The entire curriculum is delivered via a digital platform but in a consistent physical location. Students usually take traditional classes in this model as well.
- **Self-blend** Students choose to augment their traditional learning with online course work.
- **Online Driver** Students complete an entire course through an online platform with possible teacher check-ins.

All curriculum and teaching is delivered via a digital platform and face-to-face meetings are scheduled or made available if necessary.

Flipped Classroom

The flipped classroom is a pedagogical model in which the typical lecture and homework elements of a course are reversed. Short video lectures are viewed by students at home before the class session, while in-class time is devoted to exercises, projects, or discussions. The video lecture is often seen as the key ingredient in the flipped approach, such lectures being either created by the instructor and posted online or selected from an online repository. While a pre- recorded lecture could certainly be a podcast or other audio format, the ease with which video can be accessed and viewed today has made it so ubiquitous that the flipped model has come to be identified with it.

The notion of a flipped classroom draws on such concepts as active learning, student engagement, hybrid course design, and course podcasting. The value of a flipped class is in the repurposing of class time into a workshop where students can inquire about lecture content, test their skills in applying knowledge, and interact with one another in hands-on activities. During class sessions, instructors function as coaches or advisors, encouraging students in individual inquiry and collaborative effort. There is no single model for the flipped classroom, the term is widely used to describe almost any class structure that provides pre-recorded lectures followed by in-class exercises. In one common model, students might view multiple lectures of five to seven minutes each.

Online quizzes or activities can be interspersed to test what students have learned. Immediate quiz feedback and the ability to rerun lecture segments may help clarify points of confusion. Instructors might lead in-class discussions or turn the classroom into a studio where students create, collaborate, and put into practice what they learned from the lectures they view outside class. As on-site experts, instructors suggest various approaches, clarify content, and monitor progress. They might organize students into an ad hoc workgroup to solve a problem that several are struggling to understand. Because this approach represents a comprehensive change in the class dynamic, some instructors have chosen to implement only a few elements of the flipped model or to flip only a few selected class sessions during a term.

Advantages

In a traditional lecture, students often try to capture what is being said at the instant the speaker says it. They cannot stop to reflect upon what is being said, and they may miss significant points because they are trying to transcribe the instructor's words. By contrast, the use of video and other pre-recorded media puts lectures under the control of the students can watch, rewind, and fast-forward as needed. This ability may be of particular value to students with accessibility concerns, especially where captions are provided for those with hearing impairments. Devoting class time to application of concepts might give instructors a better opportunity to detect errors in thinking, particularly those that are widespread in a class.

Disadvantages

The flipped classroom is an easy model to get wrong. Although the idea is straightforward, an effective flip requires careful preparation. Recording lectures requires effort and time on the part of faculty, and out-of-class and in-class elements must be carefully integrated for students to understand the model and be motivated to prepare for class. As a result, introducing a flip can mean additional work and may require new skills for the instructor, although this learning curve could be mitigated by entering the model slowly. Students with this perspective may not immediately appreciate the value of the hands-on portion of the model, wondering what their tuition brings them that they could not have gotten by surfing the web. Those who see themselves as attending class to hear lectures may feel it is safe to skip a class that focuses on activities and might miss the real value of the flip.

Implications for Teaching and Learning

The flipped classroom constitutes a role change for instructors, who give up their front-of- the-class position in favour of a more collaborative and cooperative contribution to the teaching process. There is a concomitant change in the role of students, many of whom are used to being cast as passive participants in the education process, where instruction is served to them. The flipped model puts more of the responsibility for learning on the shoulders of students while giving them greater impetus to experiment. Activities can be student-led, and communication among students can become the determining dynamic of a session devoted to learning through hands-on work. What the flip does particularly well is to bring about a distinctive shift in priorities from merely covering material to working toward mastery of it.

Cloud Computing

Cloud computing is the delivery of computing services over the Internet. Cloud services allow individuals and businesses to use software and hardware that are managed by third parties at remote locations. Examples of cloud services include online file storage, social networking sites, webmail, and online business applications. The cloud computing model allows access to information and computer resources from anywhere that a network connection is available. Cloud computing provides a shared pool of resources, including data storage space, networks, computer processing power, and specialized corporate and user applications.

The following definition of cloud computing has been developed by the U.S. National Institute of Standards and Technology(NIST). Cloud computing is a model for enabling convenient, on-demand network access to a shared pool of configurable computing resources(e.g.,networks,servers, storage, applications, and services) that can be rapidly provisioned and released with minimal management effort or service provider interaction. This cloud model promotes availability and is composed of five essential characteristics, three service models, and four deployment models.

Characteristics

The characteristics of cloud computing include on-demand self-service, broad network access, resource pooling, rapid elasticity and measured service. On-demand self-service means that customers(usually organizations)can request and manage their own computing resources. Broad network access allows services to be offered over the Internet or private networks. Pooled resources means that customers draw from a pool of computing resources, usually in remote data centres. Services can be scaled larger or smaller; and use of a service is measured and customers are billed accordingly.

Deployment of Cloud Services

Cloud services are typically made available via a private cloud, community cloud, public cloud or hybrid cloud.

In a **Private Cloud**, the cloud infrastructure is operated solely for a specific organization, and is managed by the organization or a third party.

In a **Community Cloud**, the service is shared by several organizations and made available only to those groups. The infrastructure may be owned and operated by the organizations or by a cloud service provider.

A **Hybrid Cloud** is a combination of different methods of resource pooling (for example, combining public and community clouds).

Cloud Computing Models

Cloud Providers offer services that can be grouped into three categories.

- **Software as a Service (SaaS):** In this model, a complete application is offered to the customer, as a service on demand. A single instance of the service runs on the cloud & multiple end users are serviced. On the customers" side, there is no need for upfront investment in servers or software licenses, while for the provider, the costs are lowered, since only a single application needs to be hosted & maintained. Today SaaS is offered by companies such as Google, Salesforce, Microsoft, Zoho, etc.

- **Platform as a Service (PaaS):** Here, a layer of software, or development environment is encapsulated & offered as a service, upon which other higher levels of service can be built. The customer has the freedom to build his own applications, which run on the provider's infrastructure. To meet manageability and scalability requirements of the applications, PaaS providers offer a predefined combination of OS and application servers, such as LAMP platform (Linux, Apache, MySql and PHP), restricted J2EE, Ruby etc. Google"s App Engine, Force.com, etc are some of the popular PaaS examples.

- **Infrastructure as a Service (IaaS):** laaS provides basic storage and computing capabilities as standardized services over the network. Servers, storage systems, networking equipment, data centre space etc. are pooled and made available to handle workloads. The customer would typically deploy his own software on the infrastructure. Some common examples are Amazon, GoGrid, 3 Tera, etc.

Applications of ICT for Enriching Classroom

The pace of the society in which we live requires more flexible ways of learning and adapted to changes. Formal, non-formal, informal and invisible learning are living today in an expanded education and in a virtual space through the network. The Information and Communication Technologies are more than ever living in our society and they are important parts of the education. At Primary and Secondary Education, students start to use them in class, but the reality is that nowadays almost every student goes to school with a wide range of technological skills.

Schooling and teaching is changing with this new context. For example, students and teachers should have technological skills because they use them in their classroom and in their curricula. ICT have some characteristics that make them an essential tool in our daily life and for instance in our schools. ICT are composted of many different tools that enable capturing, interpreting, storing and transmitting information in a fast and easy way.

Main ICT´s Characteristics

Laudon and Laudon (2010) state that the most important drive behind globalization has been the explosion in Information and Communication Technologies(ICT) sectors. For these authors the main ICT´s characteristic are:

- **Mobile Learning**: New advances in hardware and software are making mobile "smart phones" indispensible tools.
- **Cloud Computing**:The implications of this trend for education systems is huge; they will make cheaper information appliances available which do not require the processing power or size of the PC.
- **One-to-One Computing**: The trend in classrooms around the world is to provide an information appliance to every learner and create learning environments that assume universal access to the technology.
- **Ubiquitous Learning**:School systems around the world are developing the ability to provide learning opportunities to students "anytime, anywhere".
- **Gaming**: The phenomenal success of games with a focus on active participation, built in incentives and interaction suggests that current educational methods are not falling short and that educational games could more effectively attract the interest and attention of learners.

- **Personalized Learning**: Education systems are increasingly investigating the use of technology to better understand a student's knowledge base from prior learning and to tailor teaching to both address learning gaps as well as learning styles.

- **Redefinition of Learning Spaces**: Schools around the world are re-thinking the most appropriate learning environments to foster collaborative, cross-disciplinary, students' centred learning.

- **Teacher-generated Open Content**: OECD school systems are increasingly empowering teachers and networks of teachers to both identify and create the learning resources that they find most effective in the classroom. Many online texts allow teachers to edit, add to, or otherwise customize material for their own purposes, so that their students receive a tailored copy that exactly suits the style and pace of the course.

- **Smart Portfolio Assessment**: The collection, management, sorting, and retrieving of data related to learning will help teachers to better understand learning gaps and customize content and pedagogical approaches.

- **Teacher Managers/Mentors**: The role of the teacher in the classroom is being transformed from that of the font of knowledge to an instructional manager helping to guide students through individualized learning pathways.

The changing role of teachers, as we saw before, is an essential part of this changing process. Their role should turn in a "guide of learning" better than in a "font of knowledge". As ICT are incorporated in education the trend of a classroom and textbook based educational system is becoming more and more outdated.

10 Reasons to Use Multimedia in the Classroom

1. Facilitate and develop a community of learners through online ice-breaker activities.
2. Help students visualize difficult concepts or procedures more easily by using static or dynamic multimedia.
3. Scaffold learning through activities enhanced by videos and online games.
4. Make language and culture come alive through the viewing and creation of audio and video instruction.
5. Provide a "menu" of authentic assignment options for students to complete, allowing them to explore and identify their passions and talents.
6. Enhance accessibility through the use of powerful multimedia software tools.
7. Enable visualization of concepts and their connections through collaborative construction and discussion of concept maps.
8. Encourage collaboration and feedback by integrating assignments with tools that support conversations and comments.
9. Make learning situated and personal with easy to access information from you and the rest of the world.
10. Help students document and present their learning through authentic assessments.

Use of Internet based Teaching and Learning

IT is a computer based technology that makes the latest information available to people almost about every field of their social, economic, political & cultural activities. CBT stands for Computer Based Training, means training through computer system. It may be used to train people in several hundred different skills from using a word processing package to learning.

Following are Some of the benefits offered by CBT

The students can study at their own pace and can repeat sections of materials that they find difficult. Some CBT products have built-in checks so that they can monitor the individual performance of each student. A major benefit of CBT for an employer is cost. The employers don't have to pay for accommodations, traveling or salaries for the trainers while the staff attends the course. The investment in the suitable training package may quickly pay for itself especially in case when suitable hardware is already available.

Through CBT staff can train when they want, often at their own desks on the computer, which they will eventually be using. Without CBT, when the new member of staff joins a company, they may have to wait until here are sufficient members to justify a course for them. With CBT, they can start on their training immediately. Real life situations can be simulated and the students or trainee can learn without the danger of performing live experiments such as Aircraft simulator.

Benefits of Computer in Education

Now a day's computers are increasingly being used in schools, colleges and other educational institutions in different areas. A computer is a great thing for a student to have, mainly because of word processing. Students can take notes in classes easier without any issues due to handwriting, or cramping.

- Greatly help to decrease their burden of work.
- Repeat a tedious process over & over for any number of times.
- Provide greater security to stored data or information.
- Produce accurate results without time consuming.

Using Computer based Learning

CAL (Computer Assisted Learning) is a package, which is increasingly being used in schools, colleges, and industries. These tutorial packages include software to teach mathematics, languages,computing, and certain other skills to instruct the users when he/she is going wrong. A series of lessons guide the user through basic features of using that particular software. No one in the modern society is unaffected by the computer. In the supermarkets, banks, libraries, hospitals, travel agencies, etc. we have their presence for granted.

Computer-based Learning in Schools

The environments in which students learn, and the ways in which people work and live, are constantly being transformed by existing and emerging technologies. To be well informed and active participants in our changing society, students will need to be self-directed learners, able to identify issues, pose questions, synthesized ideas, determine solutions to problems and develop capabilities and confidence with a range of technologies.

The first key point is that the use of computers alone will not improve learning. The advent, over the years, of other technologies, including television, the tape recorder and the overhead projector, which were each heralded as the panacea to teaching and learning, have provided us with ample evidence to support this view. We have had enough experience by now to know that technologies can be valuable tools and can transform the way we do things, but simply having access to them is not enough for students to improve their learning.

Computer-based learning needs to be driven by what students can do with the software rather than what the software provides. The critical factor in the successful introduction of computing activities into the school curriculum relates to teachers and how they ensure that learning with computers is meaningful to students.

- Learning involves the active construction of knowledge through the process of inquiry, thinking, problem solving, creating and communicating.
- Learning is purposeful. It derives from a desire to make sense of the world and act upon it.
- Learning is based on previous knowledge and requires challenges to the initial conceptions which students bring from their home and other familiar environments. The challenges lead to new insights which require students to reorganise or extend their existing framework of knowledge.
- Learning is interactive. It is more effective when students are engaged in interaction with the teacher, other students and resources, including technology.
- Learning occurs in a context of use, i.e. the situational and interactional circumstances in which knowledge is constructed and used.
- Learning is most effective when conceptual content is interrelated. It involves making connections and forming knowledge structures.
- Learning is holistic: it involves undertaking tasks as a whole rather than breaking them down into parts.
- Learning is spiral, not linear; concepts are developed at differing levels of depth and require revisiting in new contexts, thereby extending and elaborating students' frameworks of knowledge.

- Learning requires support or scaffolding. Support may be provided in instructions or through resources, including technology.
- Learning depends upon students' attitude and disposition to learning.
- Learning can be enhanced through reflecting and developing conscious awareness of patterns underlying knowledge and strategies used to activate knowledge: planning, undertaking, monitoring and evaluating action.

Course: Information Technology

It has become popular for many students to take computer-based learning courses and have found them to have more advantages than disadvantages, but believe it is an interesting topic up for discussion. A study at Iowa State University found these reasons to be among the most prevalent when discussing this topic.

Advantages of Online Computer-Based Learning

- Class work can be scheduled around work and family
- Reduces travel time and travel costs for off-campus students
- Students may have the option to select learning materials that meets their level of knowledge and interest
- Students can study anywhere they have access to a computer and Internet connection
- Self-paced learning modules allow students to work at their own pace

Disadvantages of Online Computer-Based Learning

- Learners with low motivation or bad study habits may fall behind
- Without the routine structures of a traditional class, students may get lost or confused about course activities and deadlines
- Students may feel isolated from the instructor and classmates

- Instructor may not always be available when students are studying or need help
- Slow Internet connections or older computers may make accessing course materials frustrating

Advantages of Using Computer-based Learning (CBL)

CBL provides many benefits for the organizations and individuals that set up the internal and external systems to use it effectively. Some of the benefits are listed below:

- **Available 24/7 and Just in Time:** Enables individuals to find and use the information needed exactly when they need it most.
- **Learner Controlled**: Learners know when they need additional information and for what purposes.
- **Cost-effective:** Savings occur because of the ability to use fewer instructors to reach many more learners, reduced travel expenses, reduced downtime, and the ability to train a dispersed workforce at the same time or at different levels.
- **Self-paced and User Friendly**: CBL content is becoming easier to access and manipulate.
- **Hands-on Interactivity**: CBL and other e-learning delivery approaches allow for hand- son, direct, and immediate interaction with the learning content.
- **Adjustment to Individual Learning Styles**: Adults do not all learn the same way. The variety of CBL and the different methods used to present the content appeals to different learning styles.

- **Safety and Flexibility:** The ability to simulate the actual work situations and equipment but without risk to the learner or equipment practiced on, matched with the ability to repeat the content as many times as needed.

- **Reduction of Overall Training Time:** Often, because of the consistency of content, it takes the average learner less time to complete the content delivered as CBL compared with live instructor-led training.

- **Ability to Bookmark Progress**: Learners can return and resume exactly where they left off.

- **Environmentally Friendly**: CBL reduces the use of paper and often removes the need to travel to physical classrooms.

Collaborative Technology Learning

Computer-supported collaborative learning(CSCL) is a pedagogical approach wherein learning takes place via social interaction using a computer or through the Internet. This kind of learning is characterized by the sharing and construction of knowledge among participants using technology as their primary means of communication or as a common resource. CSCL can be implemented in online and classroom learning environments and can take place synchronously or asynchronously.

The study of computer-supported collaborative learning draws on a number of academic disciplines, including instructional technology, educational psychology, sociology, cognitive psychology, and social psychology. It is related to collaborative learning and computer supported cooperative work (CSCW).

Interactive computing technology was primarily conceived by academics, but the use of technology in education has historically been defined by contemporary research trends. The earliest instances of software in instruction drilled students using the behaviorist method that was popular throughout the mid-twentieth century.

Computer-supported collaborative learning emerged as a strategy rich with research implications for the growing philosophies of constructivism and social cognitivist. The rapid development of social media technologies and the increasing need of individuals to understand and use those technologies has brought researchers from many disciplines to the field of CSCL. CSCL is used today in traditional and online schools and knowledge-building communities such as Wikipedia.

Cooperative learning, though different in some ways from collaborative learning, also contributes to the success of teams in CSCL environments. The distinction can be stated as: cooperative learning focuses on the effects of group interaction on individual learning whereas collaborative learning is more concerned with the cognitive processes at the group unit of analysis such as shared meaning making and the joint problem space. The five elements for effective cooperative groups identified by the work of Johnson and Johnson are positive interdependence, individual accountability, promoting interaction, social skills, and group processing.

CHAPTER 4

E-CONTENT DEVELOPMENT

Meaning and Concept

Normally in the growth of technology applications in education, we are moving towards a Virtual Reality where the distance between the teacher and the taught is nil. The possibility of such virtual reality can be made by generating good e-Contents and accessible by all. E- contents are basically a package that satisfies the conditions like i.e. minimization of the distance, cost effectiveness, user-friendliness and adaptability to local conditions (**Saxena Anurag, 2011**)

E-content is digital information delivered over network-based electronic devices, i.e., symbols that can be utilized and interpreted by human actors during communication processes, which allow them to share visions and influence each other's knowledge, attitudes or behaviour Towards a broader definition the design (pedagogical and learning principles used to create the digital intervention) of the subject matter and the digital delivery mode used (**NUEPA, 2007**).

It may also be defined as digital text and images designed for display on web pages. E-content means content in the electronic form. It is a combination of text, audio, video, images, animation with visual effects. Any digitized content that can facilitate the learning process and/or learning outcome can be termed as e-content. e-Content the acquisition of these contents takes place via four different channels: purchase of materials, use of freely available content on the Internet, self-production of material, exchange of existing material in a network with other institutions of Higher Education.

E-Contents should essentially be didactic in nature. The term "didactic" refers to contents such as self-instructional material, audio and video that convey some moral, fact or learning. In virtual education, the self-instructional materials are essentially didactic in nature. The philosophy behind this is that self-instructional materials try to bridge the gap between the teacher and the taught. The philosophy stands good for the e-content generation too.

According to Selinger(2004), e-content should be seen as a tool to improve the understanding, engagement and motivation of learners; to provide a safe environment for them to experiment and explore their conjectures; and to test their understanding using novel assessment methodologies based on trial and improvement; simulations and manipulation of models". The didactic nature of e-contents seems to fulfill this condition as the leaner while reading the didactic content builds an understanding and then assess that understanding using quiz/puzzles. E-Content can also be utilized as reusable learning objects. Wiley gave a working definition of learning object as "any digital resource that can be reused to support learning."

Design and Developmental Process of e-content

Unfortunately, existing materials and documents cannot be automatically transformed into e-content materials by just making them available from a Web site. A systematic and scientific approach is needed to develop quality content. Instructional Design is the teaching device that makes instruction as well as instructional material more engaging, effective and efficient. It is the branch of knowledge concerned with research and theory about instructional strategies and the process for developing and implementing those strategies. Instructional Design is the process of systematic development of instructional specifications using learning and instructional theory to ensure the quality of instruction.

There are three learning theories (Cognitism, Constructivism and Behaviourism) support the Instructional Design as backbone. Cognitism envisages the organization of the content, storing and retrieving of the content. Constructivism supports the learner centred holistic approach in e-learning. Behaviourism stresses the reinforcement, retention and transfer of knowledge in the e-Content development.

There are several approaches to explain the design and development processes of content development. Association for Educational and Communication Technology [AECT] which is a professional organization in the educational technology field in the United States, has proclaimed the five stages of instructional design that can be used to develop any learning situations and learning content, that is the ADDIE model to include Analysis, Design, Development, Implementation, and Evaluation. The ADDIE model is a basic model for designing and developing learning courses as well as educational content.

Dick, Carey, & Carey (2005) also suggest a systematic model for designing instruction and learning content, the so-called Dick and Carey systems approach model for designing instruction. The Dick and Carey systems approach model is a good guideline for designing instructional units at any educational levels.

Phase	Description	Activities	Management Issues
Planning	To determine the overall plan to develop educational content, and to identify basic information needed for development	Define the scope Identify learner characteristics Identify Learning environment Estimate time, budget and resources Produce a planning	Establish educational Standards Prepare general guidelines to plan budget Sign-off the products
Design	To conduct a primary analysis of learning tasks, and create storyboards	Develop initial content ideas Conduct goal and task analysis Prepare a planning document	Establish educational standards Prepare general guidelines to plan budget Sign-off the budget
Development	To develop all computer programs, to integrate them in one product, and to produce supplementary materials	Write program code Produce Audio and Video Assemble all pieces Prepare support materials	Make Sure for the type of delivery media and distributions conditions Sign-off the products
Evaluation	To verify the final product compared the initial plan	Do formative evaluation as an alpha test Make revisions Do a beta test Make revisions(if needed) Do summative evaluation	Arrange time and location for pilot studies Sign-off the final products

Advantages of Using E-Content

One of the most innovative and promising outcomes of distance learning and telecommunication relationship is e-learning. It is a process whereby teachers and students are linked up in an electronic media/computer network. E-content facilitates the learner in terms of any time learning, anywhere learning, asynchronous interaction and group collaboration. It provides the possibility of teaching based on learning objects. Learning objects are the smallest independent educational components which can be reused in e-content of different subjects and authors; thus it is more economical and time-saving in e-content development. The teaching method in e-learning has changed from being teacher-based to being student-based.

Virtual environment can create pervasive and dynamic interaction through virtual simulation which will upgrade learning accompanied by hearing and seeing to practical learning and experiencing.

Content is the heart of learning and medium acts as nerves in that. It requires expert knowledge in the subject area, patience in creating the necessary objects that make up quality, interactive courseware, and a high sense of creativity in structuring and sequencing the topics to make a complete whole. From this we can predict that e-Content production enriches the learning in a dynamic way. It is said that people are visual minded. They retain 20% of what they hear. 50% of what they hear and see. And probably, 100% of what they hear and see and do. This is what e-contents are poised to do and what e-contents are intended for.

Multimedia Elements of E-Content

- Text
- Graphics
- Animation
- Audio
- Video
- Menus
- Hyperlinks
- Virtual Reality

Multimedia Elements: Text

- Appropriate for the target audience.

- Easy to read.

  Serif typefaces are preferred for printed material.

  Sans serif typefaces are preferred for on-screen display.

- Formatted consistently throughout the presentation.

Multimedia Elements: Graphics

- **Graphics** are an important part of the communication process.

- They can be used to:

  - Highlight information

  - Set a mood or tone

  - Provide examples

  - Serve as backgrounds

- The two types of graphic used in multimedia are raster and vector.

- Vector graphics are made up of arcs and lines.

- Raster graphics are made of dots.

When using graphics, the multimedia designer must:

- Determine the best balance between the size and quality.

- Use appropriate graphics for the intended purpose and audience.

- Choose appropriate file formats

- Standard for the internet:

  - JPEG (Joint Photographer Experts Group)

  - GIF (Graphics Interchange file format)

  - PNG (Portable Network Graphics)

- Most popular
    - TIFF : Tagged Image File Format
    - BMP: Bitmap
    - PCX: Windows Paint
    - PICT: Macintosh
- Graphics editing programs allow designers to draw, paint, or edit images.
- A combination of different graphic programs may be used in creating multimedia presentations.

Multimedia Elements: Animation

- 2-D and 3-D animations are useful in multimedia in the areas of entertainment, education, and training.
- They can be used to create simplified illustrations of a simulation or dramatization.
- They can be much easier to understand because they are less complex than video.
- 2-D animations have smaller file sizes that video files which means quicker loading or downloading of the files.

Multimedia Elements: Sound

- **Sounds** in multimedia presentations could include:
    - Music.
    - Narrations.
    - Sound effects.
    - Original recordings.
- Sound waves are vibrations that are created when we speak.
- Sound waves are analog signals because they are continuous, fluctuating waves with no interruptions.

- Computers are digital machines, meaning that they represent data with 1s and 0s.
- To use sound on the computer, the sound waves must be converted from analog to digital form, or digitized.
- This conversion process is called sampling.

Multimedia Elements: Video

- **Videos** allow the audience to view actual events instead of just reading about or listening to them.
- Sources for videos include web sites and stock film companies.
- Videos can be used in:
    - CD-ROMS
    - Games
    - Presentations
    - Video simulations
    - Videoconferences
    - Websites.
- Videos vary in quality.

Video File Formats

- **AVI** (Audio Video Interleave)
    - Windows format, plays in Windows Media Player
    - Very good quality, even at smaller resolutions
    - Large file size – not recommended for delivering video over the Internet.
    - Popular format for videos stored on a computer.

- **MOV** (Movie)
  - Apple format, plays in the QuickTime Player
  - Very good quality
  - Popular format for videos downloaded from the Internet.
- - **MPEG** (Moving Pictures Expert Group)
  - The standard for compression and storage of audio and motion video for use on the World Wide Web.
    1. Creates video small file sizes.
    2. Popular format for videos downloaded from the Internet.
  - Its biggest advantage is that It will play in many different media players.
- **RM** (RealMedia)
  - Plays in the RealPlayer player.
  - Typically contains a movie clip.
  - Popular format for streaming video viewed over the Internet.
  - Real Player is generally supported by many different computers and operating systems.
- **WMV** (Windows Media Video)
  - Proprietary video format developed by Microsoft.
  - Plays in Windows Media Player.
  - Popular format for streaming video viewed over the Internet.
- **FLV** (Flash Video)
  - New file format widely used on the Internet.
  - Plays in Adobe Flash Player.
  - Very small file size.
  - Popular format for streaming video viewed over the Internet

Multimedia Elements: Availability

Stock clips of animation, sound, and video are: Available for free or for a fee:

- On CD's which can be purchased.
- In presentation software programs.
- On web sites.
- Made available by vendors (for sale) or individuals (created as a hobby).
- Available in several formats such as MPEG1, Quick-time or Streaming Quick-time.

Phase of E-Content Development

Design of the Development of E-Content Package

The development of E-content package consist of five phases based on research design Analysis, Design, Development, Implementation, and Evaluation of learning materials and activities.

Phase of E-Content Development

- **Analysis Phase:** Analyse phase is the foundation for all other phases of instructional design. During this phase, the investigator defines the problem, identifies the source of the problem and determines possible solutions. The phase may include specific research techniques such as need analysis, goal analysis and task analysis. The output of this phase often include the instructional goals, and a list of tasks to be instructed. These outputs will be the inputs for the Design phase.

- **Design Phase:** The Design phase involves using the outputs from the Analysis phase to plan a strategy for developing the instruction. During this phase, the investigator outline how to reach the instructional goals determined during the Analysis phase and expand the instructional foundation. Some of the elements of the Design Phase may include writing a target population, description, conducting a learning analysis, writing objectives and test items, selecting a delivery system, and sequencing the instruction. The outputs of the Design phase will be the inputs for the Development phase.

- **Development Phase:** The Development phase builds on both the Analyse and Design phases. The purpose of this phase is to generate the lesson plans and lesson materials. During this phase the investigator the constructed and developed the package with help of media software and supporting documentation. This may include hardware (e.g. simulation equipment) and software (e.g. macromedia flash).

- **Implementation Phase:** The Implementation phase refers to the actual delivery of the instruction, whether it's classroom-based, lab-based, or computer-based. The purpose of this phase is the effective and efficient delivery of instruction. This phase must promote the students' understanding of material,support the students' mastery of objectives, and ensure the students' transfer of knowledge from the learning to setting the goals.

- **Evaluation Phase:** This phase measures the effectiveness and efficiency of the instruction. Evaluation should actually occur throughout the entire instructional design process-within phases, between phases, and after implementation. Evaluation may be Formative or Summative. Formative Evaluation is ongoing during and between phases. The purpose of this type of evaluation is to improve the instruction before the final version is implemented. Summative Evaluation usually occurs after the final version of instruction is implemented. This type of evaluation assesses the overall effectiveness of the instruction. Data from the Summative Evaluation is often used to make a decision about the instruction

ADDIE Model

The ADDIE model is a framework that lists generic processes that instructional designers and training developers use. It represents a descriptive guideline for building effective training and performance support tools in five phases.

- Analysis
- Design
- Development
- Implementation
- Evaluation

ADDIE is an Instructional Systems Design (ISD) framework. Most current ISD models are variations of the ADDIE process. Other models include the Dick & Carey and Kemp ISD models. This model strives to save time and money by catching problems while they are still easy to fix. A more recent expression of rapid prototyping is SAM (Successive Approximation Model).

Instructional theories also play an important role in the design of instructional materials. Theories such as behaviourism, constructivism, social learning, and cognitivism help shape and define the outcome of instructional materials.

The model originally contained several steps under its five original phases (analyse, design, develop, implement, and evaluate). The idea was to complete each phase before moving to the next. Over the years, practitioners revised the steps, and eventually the model became more dynamic and interactive than the original hierarchical version. By the mid-1980s, the version familiar today appeared.

Analysis

The **Analyse** phase is the foundation for all other phases of instructional design. During this phase, you must define the problem, identify the source of the problem and determine possible solutions.

The phase may include specific research techniques such as needs analysis, job analysis and task analysis. The outputs of this phase often include the instructional goals, and a list of tasks to be instructed. These outputs will be the inputs for the Design phase.

Design

The **Design** phase involves using the outputs from the Analyse phase to plan a strategy for developing the instruction. During this phase, you must outline how to reach the instructional goals determined during the Analyse phase and expand the instructional foundation. Some of the elements of the Design Phase may include writing a target population description, conducting a learning analysis, writing objectives and test items, selecting a delivery system, and sequencing the instruction. The outputs of the Design phase will be the inputs for the Develop phase.

Development

The **Develop** phase builds on both the Analyse and Design phases. The purpose of this phase is to generate the lesson plans and lesson materials. During this phase you will develop the instruction, all media that will be used in the instruction, and any supporting documentation. This may include hardware (e.g., simulation equipment) and software (e.g., computer-based instruction).

Implementation

The **Implementation** phase refers to the actual delivery of the instruction, whether it's classroom-based, lab-based, or computer-based. The purpose of this phase is the effective and efficient delivery of instruction. This phase must promote the students' understanding of material, support the students' mastery of objectives, and ensure the students' transfer of knowledge from the instructional setting to the job.

Evaluation

This phase measures the effectiveness and efficiency of the instruction. **Evaluation** should actually occur throughout the entire instructional design process - within phases, between phases, and after implementation. Evaluation may be Formative or Summative.

Formative **Evaluation** is ongoing during and between phases. The purpose of this type of evaluation is to improve the instruction before the final version is implemented.

Summative Evaluation usually occurs after the final version of instruction is implemented. This type of evaluation assesses the overall effectiveness of the instruction. Data from the Summative Evaluation is often used to make a decision about the instruction

Characteristics of Multimedia Technology

Teacher education is playing a vital and crucial role in reforming and strengthening the society and is directly responsible to the development of a nation. It is an instrument which is used to change the social, economic, cultural and political system of the country. Since teacher education is system which prepares competent, talented and professionally skilful teachers which in turn produce talented individual for the development of nation. Therefore, teacher education has the most crucial position in the entire system of education. So it is imperative to pay proper attention to make teacher education more effective and successful.

Educational technologies play a fundamental role in strengthening and enhancing teaching learning process. Multimedia helps in increasing student's interest and participation in teaching learning process. Multimedia is the combination of various media used to display presentation or lectures easily. According to Rouet, Levonen, & Biardeau (2001), multimedia is defined as the combination of a variety of digital media types such as text, images, sound and video, which combine to shape an integrated multi-sensory interactive application or public presentation. Kline(1994) stated that multimedia is beneficial for pre-service teacher education programmes.

Teacher Education is a system of education, which deals with the study of teaching learning process and its application to the education of people. The main purpose of teacher education is to develop and build up an understanding of the theoretical basis of education and its role in society, and the factors, which affects teaching strategies, learning process and educational processes. It also plays a vital and crucial role in developing a plan, its implementation, in evaluation of appropriate curriculum and learning programmes.

Multimedia

The term multimedia is the set of different technologies, which are used for the purpose of communication through a combination of visual and audio media in new ways. It is used for different purposes i.e., entertainment, advertising and education. Multimedia often refers to technologies of computer. Now-a-days every PC supports multimedia because they have CD-ROM or DVD drive, a good sound card and video card usually installed in main board. However, the term multimedia also describes a number of dedicated media devices, such as Digital Video Recorders, interactive television, MP3

Players, advanced wireless devices and public video displays. Multimedia is the combination of several types of media, which consists of text, video, audio, graphics, etc. For example, a presentation, which is presented with audio and video clips, is considered a multimedia presentation.

Multi-mediation means 'many-media'. The term multimedia instructional system' refers to the applications of the set of diverse learning experiences that are presented to the students by the use of selected teaching strategies in order to strengthen one another to ensure the learners' achievement of the pre-determined and desired behavioural objectives.

Sometimes, instructional situations need the application of more than one media for the achievement of objectives. The application of more than one media aids in conveying message to the learners for all practical purposes that are not possible through single medium. Most learning events, if not all, are multi-mediated. Systematically planned, multi-mediated learning events are more predictable of product, are more effectively refineable and are easier to produce and control than single mediated learning events.

Multimedia was particularly useful in situations where there were large number of learners distributed over time and place, where learners had varied experiences and skills and where there was a shortage of teachers with subject matter expertise. Multimedia was ideal when there was a need for simulation, continuous practice or retraining; the problems of combining different learning media such as text, slides, video and audio; where subject matter was stable , and when training involved processes, procedures, problem-solving and decision making. Educational technology plays a vital role in teaching learning process and makes it more interesting, productive, effective and successful.

Multimedia Package in Teacher Training

Majority of the teachers are not trained for the effective utilization of educational technologies for instructional process. Therefore, it was necessary to train the teacher for the effective utilization of multimedia.

Suggestions to make Teacher Training a Quality

- As it was found that multimedia play a crucial role in strengthening and improving teaching learning process and help in clarifying difficult concepts easily. In addition, multimedia based teaching method increases the motivational level of the students and therefore, it is strongly recommended that all the teachers should utilize multimedia in their teaching learning process regularly.

- Availability of multimedia in our institutions is the key problem. Most of the multimedia is not available in our institutes. Therefore it should be provided to all schools on the emergency basis. Computers, multimedia, overhead projectors, educational television, radios, models, pictures, maps, flip charts, charts, film strips, educational software, flash cards etc. should be provided to all schools immediately.

- A special training programme should be introduced for the effective use of multimedia and other educational technologies. All the in-service teachers should be provided training opportunities to make them proficient in using multimedia.

- A compulsory subject regarding the preparation or utilization of multimedia should be introduced in teacher training programmes at each level so that the prospective teachers may be trained in using multimedia.

- Physical and technical infrastructure should be designed in such a way that multimedia may be used effectively.

- Special room should be constructed for keeping educational technologies.

- A special staff should be appointed by the higher authority to check the utilization of multimedia by the teachers in teachers training institutes.

- Special budget should be provided to teachers training institutes by the government to purchase multimedia and other educational technologies.

Multimedia Laboratory

Multimedia laboratory is a showroom featuring the latest multimedia technology that is hardware with software, including tools and applications. Various conditions in the developing world prevent the ready availability of such technology. The oxford dictionary defines "a resource Centre as a place where a stock or supply of materials or assets is stacked.

Meaning of Multimedia Laboratory

There are many definitions of multimedia laboratory some of us can remember when multimedia meant using a slide-tape program, where a beep signified the display of the next

35mm slide (others might remember flannel boards or 8-track tapes, but we won't go there), we will define multimedia laboratory/classroom as the integration of text, graphics, animation, sound, and/or video.

Using this very definition of multimedia, multimedia in the classroom could include Power Point presentations that are created by the teacher, commercial software (such as multimedia encyclopaedias) that is used for reference or instruction, or activities that directly engage the students in using multimedia to construct and convey knowledge. For the main purposes of multimedia has focus on engaging students in the use of multimedia to construct and convey knowledge.

Examples of Multimedia in Classroom Laboratory

- Students using concept-mapping software(such as Inspiration) to brainstorm
- Students using a spreadsheet or graphing calculator to record data and produce charts
- A small group of students creating a digital movie to demonstrate a procedure
- A class website that displays student artwork
- Students scanning their hands and importing the images into PowerPoint for a presentation about fingerprints

Functions of Multimedia Laboratory

- To provide means to integrate educational technology into the curriculum.
- To create classroom applications those are learner centered and that support high curriculum standard for all students.
- To provide students with a working knowledge of technological world.
- To develop an understanding of and capability to handle tools. Materials and processes integral to technological systems such as communications, production, power/energy and transportations system.
- To teach students to apply the knowledge, tools and skills in designing, constructing and evaluating solutions to real world technical problems.
- To facilitate design and fabricate teaching–learning material and application software need for classroom teaching.

- To select, acquire, purchase and store resources for the instructional resource Centre.
- To classify and index material for easy retrieval and condemning outdated and redundant material.

PSI

The modern world is dynamic with its revolutionary changes in all spheres of human life. Needless to mention the great changes have taken place rapidly with the introduction of educational technology the field of education and training in advanced countries of the world. The developing countries have also been imparting and adopting educational technology from the advanced countries who solve their own problem the class room communication has considerably been changed with application of education technology in teaching learning process with its emphasis on individualizing instructions.

Meaning and Concept

Personalized system of instruction (**PSI**) is the one of the recent innovation which has been successfully introduced in higher education to individualize instruction. This system of instruction which is person oriented. It is more emphasis on the individualization of instruction than other methods in higher education. The instruction is trailed to the need and ability of the individual learner. PSI get its name from the fact that each student is served as an individual by another person face to face and one to one in spite of fact that the class may contain number of students.

It is suitable for courses for the student is expected to acquire a well-defined body of knowledge or skill. The majority of college course the PSI teacher expects almost all of his students to learn his materials well and is prepared to award high grades to those, who do, regardless of their relative in the standing in the class. The teacher accepts the responsibility meeting the goal within the normal limits of manpower, space and equipment.

Objectives of PSI

The PSI has been to evolve to fulfill certain specific instructional objectives which may be enumerated has follows:

- To establish better personal – social relationship in the educational process.
- To provide frequent reinforcements for learning.
- To provide increased frequency and quantity of feed back to the instructors which the consequent benefit of a basis for meaningful revision in programme, content, and instructional procedures.
- To decrease reliance on the lecture for presentation or critical information utilizes different techniques for instructional purposes.
- To evaluate on the basis of fixed standard are mastery in a variable time period at the acceptable level of performances of the students.

Characteristics of PSI

The personalized system of instruction lays more emphasis on the importance of written works. The teacher gives practice to the learners on carefully prepared assignments consisting of section from standards text books. Articles are given to the students along with study question and other instructions as to what to read in what order and for what information. When the students things that he has mastered the materials he comes to the class room to take a brief quiz. This is immediately corrected by proctor. If there are errors the proctor indicates what part of the assignments needs further study the students goes off to do some more work and then come back to try again. That is are not examination in the normal sense. Students are not penalized for securing lower grade for an error. The specific distinctive characteristic of PSI is as follows.

- Self pacing.
- Use of multimedia.
- Use of proctors.
- Mastery learning.
- Importance of written work.

Origin and Growth of PSI

Keller created the Personalized System of Instruction (PSI) in the late 1960s in order to help students in Brazil be able to learn course material without an instructor standing by their side. Soon after, he brought his PSI program back to the United States. Due to its heavy reliance on behavioural principles, it was quickly adopted by many psychology professors and by individuals outside of psychology.

Keller(1968) outlined five basic components that he deemed to be essential for a PSI class: (1) mastery of course material, (2) the use of proctors, (3) self-pacing, (4) stress upon the written word, and (5) use of lectures and demonstrations primarily for motivational purposes.

In a standard PSI course, the course material is broken down into small units of study. The unit mastery component requires that students learn this small quantity of information and pass a test over this information by reaching some mastery criterion. If students do not reach the mastery criterion then they restudy the information and retake the unit test as many times as it takes for them to demonstrate mastery of the material.

Course credit is awarded when the unit has been mastered and there is no penalty imposed for not passing a unit test on a given attempt. The intent behind this is to reinforce test-taking attempts and mastering those tests while not punishing incorrect responses or failed attempts at mastery.

Another element in PSI is the use of proctors. Proctors, alternatively called mentors, peer reviewers, or tutors, are students who have previously mastered the material. Students can either be ones who have previously taken the course and are hired or given course credit for serving as proctors (called external proctors by Sherman, 1992), or they can be students enrolled in the course who have previously mastered a given unit of study (called internal proctors; Sherman, 1977). The proctors provide individualized feedback to PSI students about their unit test performance and often provide individualized tutoring in areas where the student is weak.

Current Status of PSI

The self-pacing feature of PSI courses allows students to move through the course material at their own pace. Thus, they can spend less time on material they understand and more time on areas they find difficult. In the initial PSI courses developed by Keller, students were not constrained by the traditional semester barriers. Rather, they could continue to work on a given course until they passed all of the unit tests.

Finally, within Keller's system the instructor is seen as the facilitator of learning rather than the person who imparts knowledge. For PSI students classroom meetings are typically used to help clarify material and motivate students to be engaged learners. The detailed learning of the material takes place outside of classroom meetings through students' active reading of the textbook and supplemental materials. Many PSI classes that use a short-answer format rely on students' answering of guided study questions from the readings.

The PSI movement once consisted of hundreds of teachers and researchers generating multitudes of publications. They had a dedicated journal and even a Centre for Personalized Instruction that served as a clearinghouse for PSI information.

Literature reviews and meta-analyses indicated that PSI was a more effective teaching method than traditional lecture methods and even the most ardent critic acknowledge the superiority of the PSI method. Many studies were conducted to determine the most efficient ways to train proctors, to reduce student procrastination, and to determine which elements of PSI were essential for the system to function effectively.

Many reasons appear to have contributed to PSI's decline from favourability. First, there were disagreements amongst PSI researchers as to what constituted a "true" PSI course. There were courses offered that upheld every tenet of the PSI philosophy and many courses that varied from Keller's prescriptions in a variety of ways. This makes it difficult to assess PSI's true effectiveness because the failure to find a result may be due to ineffectiveness of the PSI method or improper application of the PSI method. Other issues include having university administrators block PSI courses based on the belief that faculty were not actually teaching if they were not standing in front of the classroom lecturing.

Training and supervising proctors along with developing the course materials and grading multiple test attempts from each student was an onerous process and many gave this up in favour of more traditional methods. Although computer-aided PSI courses have existed since the 1980s the internet has dramatically increased the flexibility of PSI courses. Several researchers have made use of these technologies to create PSI-based programs.

Although CAPSI only allows instructors to use short-answer questions, many other programs allow for instructors to set up mastery-based multiple-choice tests. Popular course platforms such as **WebCT®** and **Blackboard®** have a mastery-based component that the instructor can use to develop a PSI component. Instructors can set the percentage that a student must attain on a given test before they are allowed to access the next test. They can also set a maximum number of attempts in order for the student to achieve mastery or dates by which mastery must be achieved.

Although it was not designed as a PSI program, it employs many of the PSI principles such as individualized instruction based on each student's performance, mastery of material, emphasis on the written word, and frequent testing over small units of material. All answers are free response format that are then marked by the computer as correct or incorrect. The computer chooses the problems presented to the student based on a series of algorithms derived from the student's incoming knowledge and mastery of previous units to determine what the student is "ready to learn."

Another solution to fitting the mastery component into a single semester is to limit the number of unit test attempts. For example, some instructors allow students to retake unit tests three or four times and take the highest grade from these attempts. The advantage of this approach is that it is likely to encourage students to study before each test attempt since they know opportunities will be limited. The drawback is that a student may not actually achieve mastery after completing the four tests.

Students with unlimited unit test attempts in a course using computer-scored multiple- choice unit tests may not go back and review during the wait time between attempts, resulting in very high numbers of attempts in order to achieve mastery. Perhaps limiting the number of attempts or using a fixed interval schedule with a limited hold for test attempts may increase more appropriate study behaviours. The conditional pass may be another way to increase critical thinking skills and student mastery of course-related material.

LCI

The thrust of discussion here involves learner control over instructional activities that are based on or delivered by a computer (including interactive videodisc, CD-ROM, and related technologies). The exploration of learner control within more traditional delivery systems-for example, the Audio-Tutorial Approach of Postlethwait, Novak, and Murray (1972) and the Personalized System of Instruction (**PSI of Keller Plan**) of F.S. Keller (1974).

Meaning and Concept

In general, "learner-controlled instruction," regardless of the instructional delivery system employed, refers to those instructional designs where learners make their own decisions regarding some aspect of the "path," "flow," or 'events" of instruction. Such an instructional process is not in any way new or novel; in fact, when examined closely, most instructional designs are seen to consist of a mixture of learner-controlled and instructor-prescribed events.

Possibilities for learner control of these types of learner-controlled activities would apply to any format of instructional delivers system. However, because the literature base focusing specifically on learner control in computer-based instructional environments is a fairly well- defined subset of studies within the larger domain of general learner control.

A supposed advantage of computer-based instruction(CBI) over more traditional forms of instruction is its capability to deliver to students "individualized" lessons. In such situations, the computer program assumes the role of manager or guide of instructional activities. In such situations, students "receive" the instruction and have little or no explicit choice over what is given.

Alternatively, the instructional computer program may abrogate such decisions and allow learners to select the instruction they are to receive. The learner operates to control the "flow" or "path" of instructional materials. Although it is certainly possible that learner choices might be afforded at a "macro" level of instruction, typically the types of instructional choices provided in computer-delivered instruction operate at the "micro" scale, that is, at the level of small instructional elements, activities, or components.

- Learning
- Time-on-Task
- Attitudes and Affect
- Effectiveness of Learner Control

Advantages and limitations

Learner-controlled instruction is, by definition, instruction in which students are required to make decisions at various points. In order to guide the design and use of learner control, it is necessary to understand the composition of such decisions: that is, can we specify the precursors and effects of the decisions.

Motivation and learner-controlled instruction are, at least in part, defined by choice activities, individual difference in motivational variables might also contribute to our understanding of the differential effects of learner-controlled instruction on learning. In contrast to attempting to specify some rationally based determinants of choice, here we need to ask if there are certain emotion-related characteristics of the students that would allow us to predict how inclined (i.e. motivated) a person is to make a particular choice. We are particularly concerned here with identifying "gut-level" predispositions, tendencies, and preferences of the students that operate to direct a choice toward one alternative or another.

CHAPTER 5

ORGANIZING AND LEARNING THROUGH ICT

Evolution not revolution, technology can have a reciprocal relationship with teaching. The emergence of new technologies pushes educators to understanding and leveraging these technologies for classroom use; at the same time, the on-the-ground implementation of these technologies in the classroom can directly impact how these technologies continue to take shape. While many new technologies have emerged throughout history, so has the cry for educators to find meaningful ways to incorporate these technologies into the classroom be it the typewriter, the television, the calculator, or the computer. And while some professional educators may have become numb to this unwavering 'call' and for good reason it is crucial to consider that the excitement over games and social networking isn't just business and industry "crying wolf." Indeed, those previous technologies have a powerful place in instruction and the classroom but without them, strong lessons and learning objectives can still be achieved.

With these more recent technologies, we think educators should take the call, even if only on a trial basis. Undoubtedly, without these recent technologies i.e. digital games, Web 2.0, etc., in the classroom, strong lessons can still be achieved, but there's a sharp disconnect between the way students are taught in school and the way the outside world approaches socialization, meaning-making, and accomplishment. It is critical that education not only seek to mitigate this disconnect in order to make these two worlds more seamless, but of course also to leverage the power of these emerging technologies for instructional gain. Of course, as a result of these assaults on formal education, those in the outside world are often quick to pounce on educators and the way education is conducted in classrooms. This bandwagon perspective has become a mounting dialogue, charging the field of education with the imperative for a revolution radical transformation of its system and practices. While it is clear that education is no different from the other sectors in its need to adapt and modify to our transforming world, it is also clear that many educators currently already implement excellent teaching practices and are able to skillfully create dynamic learning environments. Attacking educators' current practices combined with the lack of acknowledgment of current best practices only hinders the growth of the education sector.

There are countless educators who are masters at their craft, currently employing an array of exceptional instructional strategies. Lauding and building upon these strategies is critical to effective growth in the education sector in order to bridge the aforementioned divide. We advocate for an evolution in educational practices and approaches to instruction, which not only align with the processes and operations of the world outside of school, but also leverage the emerging power and potential of these new processes and technologies. Attending to this end of the technology-teaching relationship has the additional benefit of helping to shape emerging technologies that is most effective for cognition and instruction.

Patricia Marks Greenfield also argue that habitual technological utility results in the development of new cognitive abilities that translate into the key skills for our transformed world **(Facer, 2003)**

- The ability to process information very quickly
- The ability to determine what is and is not of relevance to them
- The ability to process information in parallel, at the same time and from a range of different sources
- Familiarity with exploring information in a non-linear fashion
- A tendency to access information in the first instance through imagery and then use text to clarify, expand, and explore

- Familiarity with non-geographically bounded networks of communication
- A relaxed approach to learn

It is the capacity to experiment with one's surroundings as a form of problem solving

(Jenkins, Purushotma, Clinton, Weigel & Robison, 2006).

The other side of the evolution throughout the past few decades, the emergence of new technologies has been paralleled by the evolution of theories on cognition and learning. Where learning and the mind were once viewed as filling of the bucket, the social mind is now a much more prevalent model. Of course, educators have long been aware that learning is a social activity, where learners construct their understanding not just through interaction with the material, but also through collaboratively constructing new knowledge with their peers. This collaborative learning process, where children's cognitive development is supported through the interaction and coordination of different perspectives amongst peers **(Bearison & Dorval, 2002)**, plays out in pedagogical terms as Social Constructivism. Familiar aspects of social constructivism include situated learning, where students engage in activities directly relevant and applicable to the concepts and context in which the learning will be applied **(Brown, Collins, & Duguid, 1989)** and cognitive apprenticeship, where students learn through carefully scaffolded projects where expert behavior is modeled and mediated through peer interaction. Because these pedagogies are the onramps to deep learning. Simple learning can be accessed through various methods, but acquiring complex skills requires "social interactions in situated contexts, which allows them to see how the various parts of the process fit together" **(Trent, Artiles, & Englert, 1998)**. Ill-structured domains, such as history, are particularly well-suited for the social constructivist approach, where language and co- construction of concepts is central. The collaborative, communicative, interrelated nature of the Web makes it an especially ideal tool for supporting Social Constructivism in the classroom **(McMahon, 1997)**. This may seem apparent with social networking technologies, but the powerful learning attributes of digital games and simulations are can also be enhanced when they occur online, in a networked fashion. With all of these technologies, they demonstrate their ability to be excellent tools for supporting social constructivism in the classroom not only through the real time interaction amongst classmates around the technology, but those synchronous and asynchronous interactions that occur virtually with classmates and other peer learners. Learning Theory = Teaching Practice Our innate beliefs about things like how we think people learn are often unstated, but serve as the "operating system" upon which we base our instructional decisions in the classroom. These technologies align strongly with the constructivist and social constructivist theories of learning, and therefore will also fit well into classrooms where these theories of learning are embraced. New technologies push instruction in the classroom in new ways, so our ability as professional educators push the evolution of educational technologies. With the recent tide of Web 2.0 technologies (web services which center around user-provided content, like flickr, YouTube, or Facebook), one can only speculate where things go from here. Overcoming Barriers to Innovation Groff and Mouza (2008) discuss six central factors, each with its own critical variables, that interact with one another to produce barriers to implementing technological innovations in the classroom.

- Research & policy factors
- District/school factors
- Factors associated with the teacher

- Factors associated with the technology enhanced Project
- Factors associated with the Students
- Factors inherent to technology itself.

While all dimensions are undoubtedly important, not all of them have the ability to be manipulated or accounted for by individual teachers. Research & Policy factors exist outside the district or school boundaries and, therefore, cannot be easily manipulated. The same is true for factors inherent to Technology itself. Although the characteristics of various types of technologies can facilitate or hinder efforts to use technology, teachers cannot directly influence or alter those characteristics.

Collaborative Learning and its Influences

The vast movement towards e-learning is clearly motivated by the many benefits it offers. However much e-learning is praised and innovated, computers will never completely eliminate human instructors and other forms of educational delivery. What is important is to know exactly what e-learning advantages exist and when these outweigh the limitations of the medium.

Features Unique to E-Learning

Like no other training form, e-learning promises to provide a single experience that accommodates the three distinct learning styles of auditory learners, visual learners, and kinesthetic learners. Other unique opportunities created by the advent and development of e- learning are more efficient training of a globally dispersed audience and reduced publishing and distribution costs as Web-based training becomes a standard. E-learning also offers individualized instruction, which print media, cannot provide, and instructor-led courses allow clumsily and at great cost. In conjunction with assessing needs, e-learning can target specific needs. And by using learning style tests, e-learning can locate and target individual learning preferences.

Additionally, synchronous e-learning is self-paced. Advanced learners are allowed to speed through or bypass instruction that is redundant while novices slow their own progress through content, eliminating frustration with themselves, their fellow learners, and the course. In these ways, e-learning is inclusive of a maximum number of participants with a maximum range of learning styles, preferences, and needs. All collaborative learning theory contends that human interaction is a vital ingredient to learning. Consideration of this is particularly crucial when designing e-learning, realizing the potential for the medium to isolate learners.

With well-delivered synchronous distance education, and technology like message boards, chats, e-mail, and tele-conferencing, this potential drawback is reduced. However, e-learning detractors still argue that the magical classroom bond between teacher and student, and among the students themselves, cannot be replicated through communications technology.

Advantages of E-Learning to the Trainer or Organization

Some of the most outstanding advantages to the trainer or organization are:

- **Reduced Overall Cost** is the single most influential factor in adopting e-learning. The elimination of costs associated with instructor's salaries, meeting room rentals, and student travel, lodging, and meals are directly quantifiable. The reduction of time spent away from the job by employees may be the most positive offshoot.

- **Learning Times Reduced,** an average of 40 to 60 percent, as found by Brandon Hall (Web-based Training Cookbook, 1997).

- **Increased Retention** and application to the job averages an increase of 25 percent over traditional methods, according to an independent study by J.D. Fletcher (Multimedia Review, Spring 1991).

- **Consistent Delivery** of content is possible with asynchronous, self-paced e-learning.
- **Expert knowledge** is communicated, but more importantly captured, with good e- learning and knowledge management systems.
- **Proof of Completion and Certification,** essential elements of training initiatives, can be automated.

Advantages to the Learner

Along with the increased retention, reduced learning time, and other aforementioned benefits to students, particular advantages of e-learning include

- **On-demand availability** enables students to complete training conveniently at off- hours or from home.
- **Self-pacing** for slow or quick learners reduces stress and increases satisfaction.
- **Interactivity** engages users, pushing them rather than pulling them through training.
- **Confidence** that refresher or quick reference materials are available reduces burden of responsibility of mastery.

Disadvantages to the Trainer or Organization

E-learning is not, however, the be all and end all to every training need. It does have limitations, among them

- **Up-front Investment** required of an e-learning solution is larger due to development costs. Budgets and cash flows will need to be negotiated.
- **Technology Issues** that play a factor include whether the existing technology infrastructure can accomplish the training goals, whether additional tech expenditures can be justified, and whether compatibility of all software and hardware can be achieved.

- **Inappropriate Content** for e-learning may exist according to some experts, though are limited in number. Even the acquisition of skills that involve complex physical/motor or emotional components (for example, juggling or mediation) can be augmented with e-learning.
- **Cultural Acceptance** is an issue in organizations where student demographics and psychographics may predispose them against using computers at all, let alone for e- learning.

Disadvantages to the Learner

The ways in which e-learning may not excel over other training include

- **Technology Issues** of the learners are most commonly technophobia and unavailability of required technologies.
- **Portability** of training has become strength of e-learning with the proliferation of network linking points, notebook computers, PDAs, and mobile phones, but still does not rival that of printed workbooks or reference material.
- **Reduced** social and cultural interaction can be a drawback. The impersonality, suppression of communication mechanisms such as body language, and elimination of peer-to-peer learning that are part of this potential disadvantage are lessening with advances in communications technologies.

The pro's and con's of e-learning vary depending on program goals, target audience and organizational infrastructure and culture. But it is unarguable that e-learning is rapidly growing as form of training delivery and most are finding that the clear benefits to e-learning will guarantee it a role in their overall learning strategy.

Digital Story Telling

Digital storytelling takes many forms. There are stories that are audio only and rely on words, sound effects, field recordings, and music. Hypertext environments facilitate the interactive story in which the reader chooses optional paths to explore. Web-based media facilitate not only stories with words, but also movies, stills, sounds, and graphics. People have a fundamental desire to tell each other story. Human communication seems to revolve around remembering and sharing experiences. We tell stories every day. We talk about what was and how things were done. Or we look to the future and imagine what might be. Stories are a way of sharing who we are. These personal stories often become the experiences upon which the imagination of the writer or media maker begins to weave the recreation or fictionalization of events and people as portrayed in documentaries or imaginary works in words, images, and sounds.

Stories are valuable in that they serve as a means for passing on knowledge ranging from the little things in life to those big issues which give human experience form and definition. One can define digital storytelling as the process by which people of all ages and experience share with others stories from their lives or creative imagination. This new form of storytelling has emerged with an arrival of accessible media production techniques using computers, digital cameras, recorders and software. This new technology allows individuals to share their stories over the Internet, on discs, podcasts, or other electronic distribution systems. One can think of digital storytelling as the modern extension of the ancient art of storytelling but now woven together with images and sound. With digital technologies individuals now approach storytelling from a different perspective and devise non-traditional story forms, such as non- linear and interactive narratives. There are many examples of digital stories online.

The following represent examples of material that can be found on the Internet to view and perhaps be inspired by to make one's own stores

- **Examples of Digital Stories**: Short micro movie examples from a digital story workshop in Phoenix, Arizona.

- **A History of Digital Storytelling through Story**: The Centre for Digital Storytelling has many examples of stories created during its workshops. These examples represent a history of work spanning more than a decade of practice from 1990-2003.

- **Streaming Stories**: Streaming Stories 2003 was a community of ordinary people making digital stories and films for the Internet. For six months over 100 storytellers from ten community groups all over Swindon, UK learned new skills and shared their creativity via this web site.

- **Digital Stories**: A website designed to showcase digital stories told by students and their teachers. Explore the Resources section to learn more about storytelling and using audio, video and photo tools. Go to the Video section for samples of educational, fictional, and personal digital storytelling.

- **Radio Diaries**: Since 1996, the Teenage Diaries series has been giving tape recorders to young people around the country to report on their own lives. They conduct interviews, keep an audio journal, and record the sounds of daily life. NPR works with each diarist to edit all the material into documentaries for National Public Radio's All Things Considered.

- **Fray**: The web was the ultimate conduit for personal storytelling. We saw a future web full of personal voices, where everyone has the power to tell their stories. The site was created using early web technology and it is no longer updated. However, it remains of interest to those who want to see early attempts at digital storytelling.

- **The Life of Katherine Drexel**: This story is told through the use of still images, music, and narration. It is divided into chapters. It is an example of multimedia storytelling on the web from the Philadelphia Inquirer.

- **This American Life**: Short audio stories. Each week producers choose a theme and put together different kinds of stories on that theme. They do stories that are like movies for radio, with people in dramatic situations where things happen to them.

- **Bubbe's Back Porch**: This was started in 1998 as women from around the world shared stories in real time and then posted them here to Bubbe's Back Porch. The site invites contributions of stories.

- **DigiTales:** The Art of Telling Digital Stories. Select the StoryKeeper's Gallery to access stories. These are personal stories as authored by individuals exploring digital media.

- **Bramble Town by Brent Wood**: A flash animated interactive comic strip.

- **The Ten Second Film Competition**: These published films were then rated by visitors to the site, and the top 20 user-rated films became Finalists. The Finalists were reviewed by a panel of judges, and the three winning films were announced.

- **120 Second Digital Film Festival**: A showcase for emerging filmmakers with some of the best Canadian documentaries, narratives, music videos, animated and experimental shorts.

Combining Media to Tell a Story

There are tools available online that allow you to upload pictures and audio in order to put together your digital stories. Some of the best free and online digital media storytelling tools are:

- **Storify** is an online platform that lets pull in photos, videos, text, and other social media components to tell a story. You can also drag and drop information from various sources into a timeline.

- **Meograph** is an online platform which offers one of the easiest way to create multimedia stories. It allows you to combine video, audio, pictures, text, links, maps, and timelines into your digital story. It also allows you to embed your story anywhere on the web.

- **Cowbird** if you have a few images you want to share and do not want to deal with more sophisticated digital tools, Cowbird is a fairly recent yet powerful tool for creating simple and intimate stories.

- **Popcorn Maker** Designed by Mozilla, Popcorn Maker allows you to add interactive features to videos, such as maps, photos, slides, social media, and links. It can be used for clear cut instructional videos or more creative remixes of images and sound.

- **Creativist** is an online storytelling platform that lets you incorporate text, audio, and animation to create visually attractive online stories.

- **Projqt** an online platform that lets you create dynamic multi-media presentations.

- **Zeega** is a new form of interactive media, enabling anyone to express themselves by easily combining media from the cloud and sharing these creations with the world.

Sources of Information and Learning

Education Technology has the potential to provide equal opportunities in several ways. According to **Means and Olson,** access to educational technology at school can give students from low income homes, where there is little or no access to technology, a needed edge to compete with children from more affluent homes where technology is common place in other words we can say that guaranteeing access for all classrooms to affordable educational technology in order to achieve curricular goals makes it possible to begin to address the inequities that exist among schools. **Grabe and grabe** noted that technology in the form of telecommunications allow access to people access to interactive services through online discussion groups, interactive conference and interactive tutorials and access to files through online databases, library holdings texts and graphic files on the internet.

- To understand concept of instructional resource centre.
- To design the components of instructional resources centre
- To list out necessary equipment and accessories of an instructional resource centre.

Framework for Learning Resources

The Satellite instructional Television Experiment**(SITE)** was an experimental Satellites communications project launched in India in 1975 by National aeronautics and space administration (NASA), USA and ISRO. SITE made available informational Television to rural India by various international agencies such as UNDP, UNESCO, UNICEF, ITU. It plays a major role in helping develop India's own Satellite Programe, INSAT. The programmes under the SITE were classified into 2 categories

- Educational Television (ETV)
- Instructional Television (ITV)

ETV programs mainly focused on School Children in the age group of 5-12 years. It makes the education more interesting creative purposive and stimulating and also create awareness in the changing society. ITV is mainly for adult Audience and cover incidents of national importance improved practices in agriculture, health, hygiene, family planning, Nutrition's etc. and some recreation programme.

The programmes were telecast for 4 hours each day in two transmitions. The programmes were produced after categorizing the target audience into 4 groups. Suchas Hindi, Oria, Telugu and Kannada. The SITE was operated for one fall year from August 1975 July 1976 and covered six states.

- Gain experience in the development, testing and management of Satellite based instructional TV system particularly in rural areas.
- Demonstrate the potential value of satellite technology in the rapid development of effective communication in the developing countries.
- Democrat the value of Satellite broadcast TV in thepractical instruction of village inhabitants
- Stimulate national development in India with monogerial economics technological Social implication.

Concept Mapping

Used as a learning and teaching technique, concept mapping visually illustrates the relationships between concepts and ideas. Often represented in circles or boxes, concepts are linked by words and phrases that explain the connection between the ideas, helping students organize and structure their thoughts to further understand information and discover new relationships. Most concept maps represent a hierarchical structure, with the overall, broad concept first with connected sub-topics, more specific concepts.

Definition of a Concept Map

A concept map is a type of graphic organizer used to help students organize and represent know ledge of a subject. Concept maps begin with a main idea or concept and then branch out to show how that main idea can be broken down into specific topics.

Benefits of Concept Mapping

Concept mapping serves several purposes for learners:

- Helping students brainstorm and generate new ideas
- Encouraging students to discover new concepts and the propositions that connect them
- Allowing students to more clearly communicate ideas, thoughts and information
- Helping students integrate new concepts with older concepts
- Enabling students to gain enhanced know ledge of any topic and evaluate the information

Concept Maps in Education

When created correctly and thoroughly, concept mapping is a powerful w ay for students to reach high levels of cognitive performance. A concept map is also not just a learning tool, but an ideal evaluation tool for educators measuring the growth of and assessing student learning. As students create concept maps, they reiterate ideas using their own words and help identify incorrect ideas and concepts; educators are able to see what students do not understand, providing an accurate, objective w ay to evaluate areas in which students do not yet grasp concepts fully.

Activity based Learning

Activity-based learning **(ABL)** describes a range of pedagogical approaches to teaching. Its core premises include the requirement that learning should be based on doing some hands-on experiments and activities. The idea of activity-based learning is rooted in the common notion that children are active learners rather than passive recipients of information. If child is provided the opportunity to explore by their own and provided an optimum learning environment then the learning becomes joyful and long-lasting. Activity-based learning started sometime in 1944 around World War II when a British man David Horsburgh came to India and finally decided to settle down there. He was an innovative thinker and charismatic leader. He started teaching in Rishi Valley School. Under Activity Based learning education main focus is on child or we can say that it is one of child centred approach.

It develops self-learning skill among the learners and allows a child to study according to his or her skill. Activities here can be in the form of songs, Drawings, Rhymes,Role play to teach a letter or a word, solve mathematical problems, form a sentence, and understand social science or even concept of science. The key feature of the Activity Based Learning (ABL) method is that it uses child-friendly educational aids to foster self-learning and allows a child to study according to his or her aptitude and skill. ABL serves as one model of child-centred, child-friendly education, which is the mandate of the Right of Children to Free and Compulsory Education Act **(RTE)** Act in India.

References

AECT (1972). The field of Educational Technology: A statement of definition. Audiovisual Instruction, 17, 3643.

Aggarwal, J. C. (1993). Development and Planning of Modern Education. Vikas Publishing, New Delhi. 260-261

Alessi, S. M., & Trollip, S. R. (2001). *Multimedia for learning: methods and development (3rd ed.)* Needham Heights, MS: Allyn & Bacon.

Alias, N. A., & Zainuddin, A. M. (2005). Innovation for Better Teaching and Learning: Adopting the Learning Management System. *Malaysian Online Journal of Instructional Technology*, 2(2), 27-40.

Almosa, A. (2002). *Use of Computer in Education*, (2nd ed), Riyadh: Future Education Library.

Anderson, Jonathan. and van Weert, Tom. (Eds). 2002. Information and Communication Technology in Education: A Curriculum for Schools and Programme of Teacher Development. Paris, UNESCO. http://unesdoc.unesco.org/ images/0012/001295/129538e.pdf

Anderson, Jonathan.(2010).*ICT transforming Education*. A regional guide. Bangkok: UNESCO

Andersson, A., (2008), Seven Major Challenges for e-learning in Developing Countries: Case Study e-BIT, Sri Lanka, *International Journal of Education and Development using ICT*, 4(3).

Antos, G. (2011). *Handbook of interpersonal communication*. The Hague, The Netherlands: Mouton De Gruyter.

Bekele, T. A. & Menchaca, M. P. (2008) "Research on Internet – Supported learning. A review", The Quarterly Review of Distance Education, 9(4): 373–405

Bennet, C. (2000). Preparing Teachers for Culturally Diverse Students. Journal of Teaching and Teacher Education. Vol. 16, 59

Bic, J. C., Duponteil, D., and Imbeaux, J. C. (1991).*Elements of Digital Communication*, Wiley, Chichester, UK.

Borstorff, P. C., & Lowe, S. L. (2007). Student perceptions and opinions toward e-learning in the college environment. *Academy of Educational Leadership Journal*, 11(2), 13–30.

Brown, D., Cromby, J., & Standen, P. (2001). The effective use of virtual environments in the education and rehabilitation of students with intellectual disabilities. *British Journal of Educational Technology*, 32(3), 289-299.

Chen, Y.F. & Peng, S.S. (2008) "University students' Internet use and its relationships with academic performance, interpersonal relationships, psychological adjustment, and self-evaluation", Cyberpsychology & Behavior, vol 11, 467-469

Cheng, S.-Y. & Fu, Y.-C. (2009) "Internet use and academic achievement: gender differences in early adolescence", Adolescence, 44(176),797-811

Chittaro, L. & Vianello, A. (2013) "Time perspective as a predictor of problematic Internet use: A study of Facebook users", Personality and Individual Differences, 55(8),989-993

Collins, J., Hammond, M. & Wellington, J. (1997). *Teaching and Learning with Multimedia*, London: Routledge

Davies, I., & Schwen, T. (1971). Toward a definition of instructional development, Washington: AECT.

Department for Education and Skill (2004) "Use of interactive whiteboards in history". http://publications.teachernet.gov.uk/eOrderingDownload/DfES-0812-2004 History.pdf. accessed 11 February,2007

Dick, W, & Carey, L. (2000). *The systematic design of instruction (5th ed.)*. New York: AddisonWesley.

Ely, D. (1963). The changing role of the audiovisual process: A definition and glossary of related terms. Audiovisual Communication Review, 11 (1), 1-6.

European Commission (2001). *The e-Learning Action Plan: Designing tomorrow's education.* http://www.elearningeuropa.info.

Finn, J. D. (1972). The emerging technology of education. In R. J. McBeath (Ed.), Extending education through technology. Selected writings by James D. Finn, Washington: AECT.

Fletcher, J. D. (2003). Evidence for learning from technology-assisted instruction. In H. F. O'Neil, Jr. & R. S. Perez (Eds.), Technology applications in education: A learning view. Mahwah, NJ: Lawrence Erlbaum Associates.

Fred C. Lunenburg.(2010). *Communication: The Process, Barriers and Improving Effectiveness.*

Gould, S. J. (1981). *The mismeasure of man,* New York: W. W. Norton & Company.

Graham, Charles. R.(2007).*Blended learning systems.* Definition, current trends, and future directions. In C.

Green, B.A. Jr.,(1964).The Personalized System of Instruction, Washington DC. *Journal of Aplet, Programmed Learning and Educational Technology,* V(13).

Haklev, Stian. (2008). World's largest university opens almost all its materials! Retrieved from http://reganmian.net/blog/2008/12/05/worlds-largestuniversity-opens-almost-all-its-materials/

Hannum, W.H. (2005). Instructional systems development: A thirty year retrospective. Educational Technology.

Holmes, B. & Gardner, J. (2006). E-*Learning: Concepts and Practice,* London: SAGE Publications

Indira Gandhi National Open University. (2011). Annual report, 2010–11. New Delhi: Indira Gandhi National Open University.

Kannnan.B & Muthumanickam.A., (2010), Development and Validation of E-content Package on p-block Elements for XI standard Students, Unpublished Ph.D thesis, Madurai Kamaraj University.

Keyton, J. (2011). *Communication and organizational culture: A key to understanding work experience.* Thousand Oaks, CA: Sage.

Khan BH. (2001). *A Framework for Web-based Learning.* Educational Technology Publications: Engelwood Cliffs.

Khan, B. H. (2005). *Managing E-learning: Design, Delivery, Implementation and Evaluation*, Hershey, PA: Information Science Publishing.

Klein, D. & Ware, M. (2003). *E-learning: new opportunities in continuing professional development.* Learned publishing, 16 (1) 34-46.

Kline, F. (1994). *Multimedia in Teacher education: Coping with the human element.* In J. Willis, B. Robin & D. Willis. (Eds.). Technology and Teacher Education Annual, 1994.Charlottesville, VA: Association for the Advancement of Computing in Education. pp. 759-763.

Kneen, J. (2011). *Essential skills: Essential speaking and listening skills.* New York, NY: Oxford University Press.

Mayer, R. E. (2001). *Multimedia Learning.* New York: Cambridge University Press.

Mooij, T. (2007), 'Design of educational and ICT conditions to integrate differences in learning: Contextual learning theory and a first transformation step in early education', Computers in Human Behaviour. 23(3),1499--1530.

Morrison, Gary R.(2010).*Designing Effective Instruction*, 6th Edition. John Wiley & Sons.

NCERT.(2006).National Focus Group On Educational Technology. New Delhi: Publication Department, NCERT: New Delhi

Nicholson, J., Nicholson, D., & Valacich, J. S., (2008) Examining the Effects of Technology Attributes on Learning: A Contingency Perspective. *Journal of Information Technology Education*, Vol 7, Retrieved from http://www.jite.org/documents/Vol7/JITEv7p185204Nicholson364.pdf

Pagram, P., & Pagram, J., (2006), "Issues in e-learning: A Thai Case Study", _The Electronic Journal of Information Systems in Developing Countries_, 26(6),1-8

Pelgrum, W. J., Law, N. (2003) _"ICT in Education around the World: Trends, Problems and Prospects"_. UNESCO-International Institute for Educational Planning.

Pelgrum, W.J. (2001)._Obstacles to the integration of ICT in education: results from a worldwide educational assessment._ Computers & Education, 37(2),163–178.

Richad Kolothumthodi (2008), Development and Validation of E-content package on communication: Process and Type for the B.Ed. Trainees. Unpublished M.Ed. dessertaion, Barathidasan University, Tiruchirappalli.

Ruskin, R.S., _The Personalized System of Instruction._ An Educational Alternative ERIC Higher Education Report No.5, Washington DC

Sharma, R. (2003), _'Barriers in Using Technology for Education in Developing Countries'_,IEEE0-7803-7724-9103.Singapore schools', Computers & Education.41(1),49-63.

Stoddart, T., & Niederhauser, D. L. (1993). "Technology and educational change. Computers in the Schools", No. 9,5–22.

Susman, E. B. (1998). "Co-operative learning: a review of factors that increase the effectiveness of computer-based instruction". _Journal of Educational Computing Research_, 18(4), 303–322.

The Hindu (Chennai, 2004)."_Where mind is without fear_".

Valentina Arkorful & Nelly Abaidoo(2014). The role of e-learning, the advantages and disadvantages of its adoption in Higher Education. _International Journal of Education and Research._ 2(12)._ISSN: 2201-6333 (Print) ISSN: 2201-6740 (Online)_

Vallikkad, S. (2009). _Information & Communication Technology for Teacher Education._ New Delhi : Kanishka Publishers & Distributors.

Venkataiah, N. (1996). Educational Technology. New Delhi: APH Publishing Corporation

Wheeler, S. (2001). Information and communication technologies and the changing role of the teacher. *Journal of Educational Media*, 26(1),7-17.

http://timesofindia.indiatimes.com/city/kolhapur/Activity-based-learning-to-be-introduced-in-200-moreschools/articleshow/38019841.cms

www.Erics.co.in

www.e-learningguru.com/

www.educational.com

http://www.ehow.com/list_6610785_advantages-using-internet-university education.html

http://www.ehow.com/facts_5549217_advantages-internet-education.html